Make it
Moroccan

MODERN CUISINE FROM THE PLACE WHERE THE SUN SETS

Make it
MOROCCAN

MODERN CUISINE FROM THE PLACE WHERE THE SUN SETS

HASSAN M'SOULI

NEW
HOLLAND

DEDICATION

I would like to dedicate this book to my dad and my sisters.
My hard-working dad whose blessing truly protects me and my
sisters who kept me on the right path, taking over after
my mother passed away, always believing in me.

ACKNOWLEDGEMENTS

I would firstly like to thank my loyal customers of Out of Africa Restaurant and everyone from Australia to Luxembourg who bought a copy of *Moroccan Modern*, for without you there would be no success and this book would never have happened.

I want to thank my dedicated staff at the restaurant; Fuad Mahboub, Dan Johnson, Katsu Kawamura, and Dai Shibata for keeping the kitchen bustling and showing such passion throughout.

Thanks to Zoe Slatyer and Alex Mancini who took care of managing the restaurant with vibrancy and care so that I could keep my head in this book.

I sincerely thank my wife Najma who searched through French, Arabic and Spanish writings until late at night to help make this book so special and also my daughter Jasmine who helped me get my thoughts and ideas down on paper and went through the pages with me to get it just right. Thank you both for your support in sharpening this book to what it is, without you it would not be complete.

To my son Ramahl, thank you for your understanding. I value my time with you so I really appreciate your patience.

Thank you to my best friend Omar Majdi from Souk in the City restaurant for your friendship and support for as long as I can remember.

Thanks to my brother Semo, you've always been there for me, with understanding and support.

Thanks as well to Rashid from Ambience and everyone who has contributed to the settings and equipment I used to show the traditional and authentic attributes of Moroccan cuisine.

Of course I thank New Holland Publishers for your faith and trust in me; my brilliant publisher Fiona Schultz for your encouragement, professionalism and great ideas and the whole team whose dedication made this book happen, including Publishing Manager Lliane Clarke, Designer Hayley Norman and talented photographer Graeme Gillies.

Thank you to anyone who I've missed, to everyone and anyone who has helped in any way, you know who you are.

And thanks to all of you who choose this book. Your interest in Moroccan food truly makes me proud.

CONTENTS

Map of Morocco   11

MOROCCO
Land of spices   13

KHOBZ & PASTILLA
Bread and pastry   31

ARGAN OIL
Uniquely Moroccan   43

BRUSCHETTA & DIPS
Delicate flavours   51

TAJINES
Breakfast tajines   65
Main course tajines   79

COUSCOUS
Happiness and abundance   97

HARISSA
Infused and aromatic   109

SPICES
Zaatar, Ginger, Dukkah and Ras el Hanout   121

PRESERVED LEMONS & LIMES
A Moroccan citrus classic   131

SAFFRON
Precious gold   141

SALADS
Fresh and colourful   157

ARTICHOKES
Wild heart   171

POMEGRANATES
Ancient fruit   179

DESSERTS
From brûlée to blossom shots   189

DRINKS
Mint tea, Arabic coffee and wine   209

SPAIN

Strait of Gibralter

Mediterranean Sea

Tangier
Asilah
Tetouan

Oujda

Atlantic Ocean

Rabat

Fes

Casablanca

Meknes

Bouarfa

Safi

Marrakech

Atlas Mountains

Er Rachidia

Essaouira

Ziz Valley

Taroudant

Mt. Toubkal

Erfoud

Agadir

Tinehir

Canary Islands (Spain)

Ouarzazate

Merzouga

Tiznit

Draa Valley

Tafrout

Zagora

ALGERIA

Tan–Tan

Laayoune

Samara

Cabo Bojador

Bu Craa

Guelta Zemmur

Ad Dakhla

WESTERN SAHARA

Bir Gandus

MOROCCO

MOROCCO
LAND OF SPICES

Morocco's compelling allure comes from its distinctive fusion of traditional and modern culture, exquisite art, remarkable architecture and stunning landmarks which offer rich and enlivening experiences that entice all the senses. Moroccan food has been enriched for over two thousand years by surrounding cultures to become a unique mix of sweet, salty, earthy spice flavours that I find the richest in Eastern cuisine.

Morocco is the gateway between Africa and Europe; the cuisine itself is a blend of the traditional and of the colonial and trade influences and quite dissimilar to the herb based recipes on the other side of the Mediterranean Sea. Moroccan cooking is distinguished by rich spices. Saffron, coriander, cinnamon, chillies, cumin, ginger and paprika are the most commonly used.

Marrakech is a city of art. It represents a very important element of Moroccan culture, the blend of the old and the new, the traditional and the refined. The flavours of Marrakech are essentially saffron, parsley, cloves, mint and the traditional ras el hanout (head of the shop)—a mixture of twenty seven spices, although it can use up to a hundred depending on who makes it. No two blends are exactly alike. Marrakech is my mother's birthplace and a city of markets and festivals. The food is always a cause for celebration with elaborate dishes that treat the senses.

'TO MY MIND FOUR THINGS ARE NECESSARY BEFORE A NATION CAN DEVELOP A GREAT CUISINE. THE FIRST IS AN ABUNDANCE OF FINE INGREDIENTS, A RICH LAND. THE SECOND IS A VARIETY OF CULTURAL INFLUENCES: THE HISTORY OF THE NATION, INCLUDING ITS DOMINATION BY FOREIGN POWERS, AND THE CULINARY SECRETS IT HAS BROUGHT BACK FROM ITS OWN IMPERIALIST ADVENTURES. THIRD, A GREAT CIVILIZATION, IF A COUNTRY HAS NOT HAD ITS DAY IN THE SUN, ITS CUISINE WILL PROBABLY NOT BE GREAT; GREAT FOOD AND A GREAT CIVILIZATION GO TOGETHER. LAST, THE EXISTENCE OF A REFINED PALACE LIFE, WITHOUT ROYAL KITCHENS, WITHOUT A VERSAILLES OR A FORBIDDEN CITY IN PEKING, WITHOUT, IN SHORT, THE DEMANDS OF A CULTIVATED COURT, THE IMAGINATIONS OF A NATION'S COOKS WILL NOT BE CHALLENGED. MOROCCO, FORTUNATELY, IS BLESSED WITH ALL FOUR.'

—PAULA WOLFERT, EASTERN CUISINE SPECIALIST AND AUTHOR

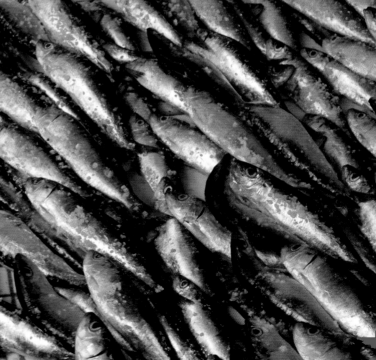

In the past it took a few people who were passionate about food to continue the long-standing traditions and keep a record of traditional recipes in **Fez**. These recipes come from an Andalusian background and are characterised by cumin, cinnamon, paprika, ginger and coriander. The most well known local dish is chicken tajine sweetened with prunes.

The laid-back medina town of **Essaouira** seduces its visitors with its sense of peace and tranquility. This much loved town is trying hard to remain a well kept secret. It shows a different side of Morocco—walking around you can see the 18th century Portuguese architecture as the salty sea winds fill the town from the curving sandy beaches and fishing bays.

The seaside town of **Agadir** was the first sardine seaport in the world. Walking through the town, you can watch the fishermen repairing their nets and drawing in the seafood for the day; sardines, whiting, tuna, shrimp, crabs, lobster and prawns: while once home to a German colony, this town has stayed true to its culinary roots with dishes traditionally prepared with almonds, cinnamon and honey sprinkled with argan oil.

Erfoud is a small town on the river Ziz in the south of Morocco, just on the edge of the Sahara desert. It was built during the French occupation in the 1930s as the administrative centre for the country's biggest oasis.

Nearby is **Merzouga** the gateway to the magnificent sand dune Erg Chebbi, and to **Tinerhir** with its stunning Todra Gorge. When you visit Morocco you can't miss the Merzouga sand dunes. Believe me, the early wake up call before sunrise is more than worth it for the amazing experience of watching the sun as it rises from the top of the shimmering gold dunes and riding a camel back to the Sahara tents for a special breakfast with the Touargees people, followed by a day in the holy ancient city of Rissani and the ruins of Sijilmassa, exploring the old caravan routes from the 8th century. The town of Erfoud is a place I truly adore, a place like no other.

The capital of Northern Morocco, **Tetouan** is situated in the midst of greenery. A belt of orchards planted with orange, almond, pomegranate and cypress trees surround dazzlingly white houses that cling to the Dersa and Ghourghiz hillsides. The scents of the fresh blossoming fruits fill the city and inspire beautiful cakes and delicate pastries.

The capital of Morocco **Rabat** is the political, industrial, cultural, artistic and educational centre of the country. The city is modern while still boasting old palaces and streets. King Hassan originally set up the cooking school *Centre de Qualification Hotelière et Touristique de Touarga-Rabat* for the daughters of the palace as a way to maintain the authenticity of Moroccan cuisine, but soon the school expanded and is now open to all as long as you can pass a tough exam to get in. Rabat is the base for the Royal Moroccan kitchen cuisine.

The food of **Casablanca** recreates the lost world of the *pied noir*, the French colonists of North Africa, and is a perfect example of food reflecting a variety of cultures. Borrowing ingredients from their Arab neighbours, the *pied noir* cooked meats with fresh fruits such as lamb with pear and chicken with quince. Salads combined European vegetables with North African spices such as beetroot and carrot salad with cumin. Casablanca is my city and when I think of it I'm reminded of the smells and sounds of a busy city and the tastes I grew up with. Twice a day we would carry homemade dough to the *ferrain*, a large local communal underground oven where the baker would cook it and we would come back later to pick it up. Growing up food wasn't just food, it was a part of my culture and meal times were a time for the family to all be together, a true blessing amongst the hard times.

Moroccan food is about sensuality, it appeals directly to the senses of smell, sight and taste in a way that no other culture has mastered. It's well known amongst Moroccans that the best meals are found at home. It's not expert chefs from Fez, Meknes, Marrakech and Rabat that define Moroccan cuisine, but the food being cooked in the home. Whether it be for lunch or for a wedding feast these meals are what we know as Moroccan cuisine today. Much loved dishes are of course couscous served with a variety of meat and vegetables; *mechoui*, roasted lamb; *djej emsharmel*, a roast chicken dish cooked with lemon and olives and *bi'stilla*, a delicious savoury and sweet pastry dish.

Raw ingredients in Morocco are proudly home grown; olives and mint come from **Meknes**, citrus fruits from **Fez** and prickly pears from **Casablanca.** Almonds, dates, chestnuts, walnuts, cherries, melons and pomegranates are grown throughout the country. The Atlantic coast supplies Morocco's seafood markets and the countryside provides lamb and poultry.

Moroccan food is all about spices. Ground dried ginger, cumin, salt, black pepper and turmeric are found in almost every dish. Cumin is an essential in Moroccan cuisine and is usually served on the table along with salt and pepper. Cinnamon is found in tajines, desserts and pastry dishes. Paprika and chilli are used to spice up vegetable dishes and for marinating meat. Saffron is grown in the south of Morocco and not only used in food but also in tea and as a herbal medicine. Cardamom is often used in creamy dessert dishes and cakes. Sesame seeds are used on pastries and sweet meat dishes, it is a very important ingredient during Ramadan in the traditional desserts.

You always buy both parsley and coriander at the markets, they are the most commonly used herbs in Moroccan cuisine, important to almost every dish. Next is mint, essential in Morocco for mint tea. Anise and thyme are often used on pastries and bread and baked or roasted fruit, like figs and apricots.

Moroccans love olive oil. The rich land is great for growing olives although export has made the product almost too expensive for the average Moroccan family and most households now resort to using vegetable oil. Argan oil is a stronger, richer oil grown in the south which is used in salad dressings, in desserts and as a health and beauty product.

Wherever you visit in Morocco you will be surrounded by a bustling atmosphere vibrant with travelling entertainers, traders and mischievous children. This is what draws the visitor into the exciting life of Morocco. When I travel to the mountains, the city commotion subsides and the calm and tranquil sounds of nature, native birds, waterfalls and the wind rustling the olive branches take over. I can smell the beautiful scent of jasmine and rose that hangs in the air and my senses become attentive to the aromatic scent of mint tea and fresh ground spices that endure in my memory, remind me of my culture, create experiences for me to share and inspire my cooking.

KHOBZ & PASTILLA
BREAD & PASTRY

'MANAGE WITH BREAD AND BUTTER UNTIL GOD SENDS HONEY.'

—A MOROCCAN PROVERB

Bread is the staple at every Moroccan table for every meal, *the* most important food in the traditional way of life. Bread in Morocco is not just a staple it's almost sacred, a symbol of sharing and harmony, the bearer of *baraka*, good fortune. To Moroccans, bread is to be appreciated, savoured and never wasted—bread seen lying on the ground is picked up, given a blessing and placed somewhere clean.

Bread is eaten with every meal as a fork and for mopping up sauces and is always handed out by one person at the table to prevent arguing. We love it hot in the morning with olive oil, dates, honey and a bit of cheese and a glass of mint tea. It makes a complete meal for a farmer or shepherd out in the country.

I remember as a kid, every morning before my dad left for work he would eat just hot bread made from barley flour with olive oil and that was his simple breakfast. He used to say with his mouth half full, 'this will make you strong' then drink half a glass of the olive oil too, as his father did before him.

There are so many different types of bread in Morocco. *Kesra*, country bread, is the most common and the most familiar to me. It's usually made from a mix of unbleached flour and whole wheat, barley or cornflour and shaped into flattish round loaves.

Each and every morning my family would make our dough, mark it, then take it in to town to be baked in the communal wood fire oven. Each household would add their favourites to the dough such as cumin, sesame, aniseed grains or caraway seeds. During festivals and special ceremonies my mother always added caraway seeds and cinnamon for a sweeter bread.

KHOBZ

MOROCCAN BREAD

KHOBZ
MOROCCAN BREAD

3 teaspoons active dry yeast
2 teaspoons sugar
2 teaspoons salt
2½ cups lukewarm water
500g (1lb) plain flour
500g (1lb) fine wheat semolina
½ cup vegetable oil
2 teaspoons caraway
1 tablespoon anise seeds seeds

Preheat the oven to moderately hot, 200°C (400°F) Gas Mark 5.

Dilute the yeast, sugar and salt in a bowl with ½ cup of the lukewarm water and set aside for 10 minutes.

Sift the flour and semolina into a large shallow dish. Make a well in the centre, pour in the yeast water and mix together.

Add 1 cup of the water and half the oil and knead vigorously. The dough should be soft and elastic, if you don't think it will be soft enough add more warm water, 1 teaspoon at a time.

Add the caraway seeds and then knead for a further 10 minutes. The dough is ready if it bounces back when you press down with your finger.

Divide the dough into four equal balls, place them on a clean floured surface, brush with a little of the leftover oil then flatten each ball into a disc.

Sprinkle with anise seeds and allow to rise in a warm place under a tea towel away from any draught for 1½ hours or until it doubles in size.

Bake for 15 minutes then turn the oven down to slow, 150°C (300°F) Gas Mark 2 for another 20 minutes or until golden brown.

For crustier bread, turn upside down and bake for a further 5 minutes.

MAKES 4 LOAVES

R'FISSA BE REZAT EL KADI
TURBAN OF THE JUDGE

TURBAN OF THE JUDGE

1 whole chicken, size 14

Marinade
1 clove garlic, crushed
¼ cup olive oil
½ tablespoon ground ginger
½ tablespoon ras el hanout (see page 124)
1 teaspoon salt
1 teaspoon ground black pepper

Rezat el Kadi (pastry)
1kg (2lbs) plain flour
2 teaspoons salt
2 teaspoons sugar
2 cups water
Vegetable oil

5 cloves garlic

R'fissa sauce
¼ cup olive oil
2 large onions, chopped
1 teaspoon ginger
1 teaspoon ras el hanout (see page 124)
½ tablespoon zaatar
1 teaspoon salt
1 teaspoon ground black pepper
2 tablespoons prepared saffron (see index)
1 bunch coriander
1 bunch parsley
1½ litres (2½ pints) chicken stock
1 cup dry lentils
1 tablespoon fenugreek seeds,
   soaked overnight
2 tablespoons blue cheese, mixed with warm
   water to achieve a creamy paste

Run the chicken under cold water to wash it, then place it in a bowl. Combine the marinade ingredients and rub them in to the chicken. Leave it in the fridge for at least 2 hours to marinate.

In a large bowl, mix the flour, salt and sugar together and pour in enough of the water to form a stiff dough.

On a clean dry surface, knead the dough for about 10 minutes until it is smooth. Divide into walnut sized balls. Coat each ball with oil.

Ensure your hands and working surface are well oiled before rolling out each ball of pastry with your fingertips until it is stretched out and as thin as paper, alternatively you can place the dough through pasta machine rollers.

Feed the thin pastry sheets through a pasta machine to shred them into very thin strips.

Take a ball's worth of strips, pinch and twist the strips into a spiral, they will end up looking like a turban or a nest. Repeat for each lot of shredded pastry.

Ensuring each pastry cake is well oiled, heat a large fry pan without oil and place each one in the pan. You will need to do this in batches. Cook the pastry cakes on both sides until you have golden brown spots appearing. Take out of the pan and set aside.

Preheat the oven to moderate, 180°C (350°F) Gas Mark 4.

In a large saucepan, heat a dash of olive oil over medium heat and brown the chicken for about 10 minutes.

Place the chicken in a baking dish with half a cup of water, cover and roast for 15 minutes.

Remove the cover and add the garlic, then roast for another 10 minutes at moderately low 160° C (325°F) Gas Mark 3.

Take out the chicken, leaving the garlic cloves in the oven with the heat off to keep them warm for later.

Make the sauce in a large pot (preferably one with a steamer to place on top). Heat the olive oil, fry the onions, ginger, ras el hanout, zaatar, salt, ground black pepper, prepared saffron, coriander and parsley. Add the chicken stock and simmer uncovered for about 10 minutes over medium heat.

Then add in the lentils, fenugreek and blue cheese. Place the lid on and cook for about 20 minutes or until the lentils are tender, add more salt if you need it.

Place the pastry cakes in the top of a couscoussier or a steamer over the sauce until they are warm and soft.

To serve, place the pastry cakes on the bottom of a large deep serving dish. Pour over a sufficient amount of sauce, place the roast chicken on top in the middle and garnish with the roasted garlic cloves.

Serve any remaining sauce in a bowl on the table for people who would like more. Enjoy.

SERVES 4–6

TRID BE RGHAIF

TRID BE RGHAIF
TRID BE RGHAIF

2 tablespoons olive oil
1.4 kg (2¾lbs) chicken, cut into 6 pieces
1 tablespoon salt
1 tablespoon pepper
2 bay leaves
½ tablespoon ground ginger
Saffron threads, pinch
½ tablespoon yellow food colouring powder
2 tablespoons fenugreek seeds, having had soaked in water overnight
1 stick cinnamon
2 large brown onions, sliced
100g (3½oz) *smen* (aged butter) or blue cheese,
   or butter if you can't take the scent
1 cup of fava (broad) beans, dried
100g (3½oz) almonds, crushed and roasted
½ bunch coriander (cilantro)
½ bunch parsley

Rghaif (Dough)
250g (8oz) wholemeal flour, sifted
250g (8oz) fine plain flour, sifted
½ tablespoon salt
Oil

Mix the flours and the salt in a large bowl, slowly pouring in enough water to make a bread-like dough. Keep the dough soft, still very elastic and easy to handle.

Roll into a ball and cover in oil, flatten and shape into rings placing one on top of the other and pressing down the edges with your thumbs, making sure it's well oiled in between.

Flatten further with your fingertips until as thin as pancakes.

Deep fry in a pan of hot oil until cooked through. Allow to cool.

Separate the two sheets of pastry. Roll each sheet up and cut in to strips 1cm (½in) wide with scissors.

Heat the oil in the pot of a large *couscousier* or pan with a steamer and put in the chicken pieces, salt, pepper, bay leaves, ginger, saffron and colour, fenugreek, cinnamon and the onions.

Cook for 5 minutes on a low heat, stirring constantly until the chicken is browned.

Stir in the *smen* cover with 1½ litres (2½ pints) of water and simmer for 15 minutes.

Add the fava beans with another litre (1¾ pints) of water.

Cook for another 20 minutes until the sauce is reduced to a thick consistency.

Once all cooked, place the steamer on top and put in the *rghaif* pieces. Steam for 5 minutes so that they absorb the flavours of the chicken and spices as they cook.

Transfer the *rghaif* to a large serving dish and top with the chicken and half the sauce.

Garnish with the almonds.

Tie the coriander and parsley together with string and soak in bowls of the remaining sauce and serve as a side dish for those who would like more.

SERVES 4–6

PASTILLA BELKHODRA
VEGETABLE PASTILLA

½ tablespoon butter
100g (3½oz) potato, washed and diced
50g (2oz) carrot, washed and diced
50g (2oz) cabbage, washed and diced
50g (2oz) zucchini (courgette), washed and diced
1 teaspoon salt
1 teaspoon white pepper
20g (¾oz) leek, chopped
5g (1/6oz) chopped coriander (cilantro)
100g (3½oz) spring roll pastry
1 egg, whisked
Olive oil for deep-frying
10g (1/3oz) mint leaves, to garnish

Melt the butter in a saucepan and sauté the potato, carrot, cabbage and zucchini.

Season with salt and pepper and add the leek.

Add coriander and turn off the heat.

Cut the spring roll pastry into circles.

Fill each sheet with the sautéed vegetables, roll up and tuck the ends in like a spring roll and seal with the egg.

Deep fry.

Drain on paper towels before transferring to a plate, garnish with mint leaves and serve hot.

SERVES 2

I was first introduced to this dish on a trip to Erfoud. Some local friends took me a town called Rissani where we selected a some meat from the local butcher and mixed spices and herbs from the market and took them to the town's traditional 'baker'. The bakers placed our mixture into the centre of some dough and sealed it with another piece, marked it then took it to be cooked in the large communal oven. It was an unusual experience and one I was glad to have tried.

This recipe originally comes from the south where they would light a fire in the desert then extinguish the flame and bury the filled dough in the hot sand to cook. For this recipe we will be realistic and use an oven!

MEDFOUNA
BERBER-STYLE PIZZA

Dough
2 teaspoons active dried yeast
175ml (5½fl oz) lukewarm water
250g (8oz) plain flour
1 teaspoon caraway seeds
½ teaspoon salt

1 tablespoon argan oil
1 teaspoon thyme leaves, no stalk
Pink salt flakes for topping, pinch

Filling
500g (1lb) fillet steak, finely chopped
1 cup charmoula
½ cup of parsley leaves
½ cup fresh coriander leaves
½ cup dried black olives, pitted and halved
4 soft boiled eggs, sliced

Pre-heat the oven to moderate, 180°C (350F) Gas Mark 4.

To make the dough, mix the yeast with the water until it dissolves.

Combine the flour, caraway seeds, salt and yeast water in a bowl, lightly flour your work bench and knead the dough for 10 minutes.

Split the dough in half and place each equal half in a bowl. Using plastic wrap or a tea towel, cover the bowls and leave in a warm place for half an hour to rise, or until the dough doubles in size.

For the filling, combine the meat, charmoula, parsley and coriander in a bowl, mix well.

Roll out each half of the dough to the size of a dinner plate. Place one dough disc on a baking tray and top with first the olives and sliced egg and then the meat mixture, spreading it evenly and leaving a 2cm (¾in) edge which you brush lightly with water.

Place the second piece of dough on top, press down the edges to seal and slightly turn them up to make a crust.

Flip the filled dough (upside down so it looks better) on to a lightly greased baking tray.

Brush the top with the argan oil and sprinkle over the thyme leaves and salt.

Place in the oven and bake for about 20 minutes then turn off the heat and leave for another 10 minutes until golden brown.

Serve on a large plate and cut into slices.

SERVES 4

ARGAN OIL

UNIQUELY MOROCCAN

Cherished for centuries by Moroccan Berbers argan oil has now captured the attention of the modern world. A recent issue of *The New York Times* boasts, 'this...might even eclipse white truffle oil in the drizzle department'.

Argan oil comes from the nut of the argan tree (*Argania spinosa*) which is relatively unknown because it only grows in a small area in the south west of Morocco where it is perfectly adapted to the arid conditions. It is very hardy and can live from 150 to 200 years. Its roots grow deep in search of water and thus help retain the soil, prevent erosion and limit the advance of the desert. It plays a vital role in maintaining the ecological balance and the economic situation of the population of the area. In 1999, UNESCO added the tree to the World Heritage List because in less than a century more than a third of the argan forest has disappeared.

The fruits of the argan tree are green. They look like an olive but are larger and rounder. Inside, there is a hard-shelled nut which can contain up to three kernels from which the nutritious argan oil is extracted. The leftovers from this process are used to feed cattle and the shells are used for heating. Nothing is wasted.

Oil production is a demanding and laborious process which was until recently completely performed by hand. First the nut was extracted from the fruit then cracked to collect the kernels. These were roasted and once cooled, ground in a stone rotary quern. The kernels were then hand-mixed with water to form a dough from which the oil was extracted by hand, although recently mechanical presses have been introduced which considerably reduce production time. However, the most time consuming part of the process, cracking the nuts, is still done by hand.

The oil is cold pressed, slightly darker than olive oil and has a nutty flavour and a high nutritional value. In the Berber tradition, it plays an important role in the preparation of meals, either used plain and pure, with bread or in seasonings. It is used in salads, tajines and couscous, to marinate roasted peppers and tomatoes and to enhance semolina dishes. It also features in the preparation of *amlou*, a delightful treat to serve guests which is reputed to have aphrodisiac qualities!

Recently, argan oil has entered European cuisine, introduced by chefs inspired by its usual flavour. Internationally it has also gained attention for its cosmetic and nutritional properties. It contains Omega 6 and is also rich in tocopherols which work like vitamin E, the most powerful anti-oxidant. The Moroccan pharmacopoeia also recommends it for acne, burns, and chapped skin. Numerous laboratories are now using this oil in a wide range of products.

A fantastic winter vegetable dish.

GRILLED POLENTA WITH GLAZED PARSNIP AND PUMPKIN SAUCE

GRILLED POLENTA WITH GLAZED
PARSNIP AND PUMPKIN SAUCE

6 cups cold water
1 teaspoon salt
2 cups yellow cornmeal
2 tablespoons argan oil
50g (2oz) Parmesan, grated

Glazed Parsnips
4 large parsnips
¼ cup brown sugar
¼ cup (60ml/2fl oz) apple cider

Pumpkin Sauce
1 small butternut pumpkin,
   peeled and de-seeded (pitted)
2 tablespoons argan oil
1 teaspoon pink salt
4 cloves garlic, not peeled
2 tablespoons harissa
Vegetable stock, optional
Coriander leaves, to garnish

To make the polenta, combine the water, salt and cornmeal in a pan over low heat, then boil for 20 minutes and set aside for another 20-30 minutes until it becomes thick.

Pour into a 2cm (¾in) deep square oven tray lined with baking paper.

Brush with oil, sprinkle with cheese and place under the grill for 5 minutes or until golden brown.

Once cooked, cut into 6 even squares, ideally 9cm by 9cm (3½in x 3½in).

Preheat oven to moderate, 180°C (350°F) Gas Mark 4.

Wash the parsnips in cold water, and cut off the very end and the very top of the parsnip and cut in half lengthways.

Mix the brown sugar and apple cider together in a bowl and marinate the parsnips for 15 minutes.

Place on a baking tray and bake for 15 minutes.

Cut pumpkin into 3-4cm (1-1½in) cubed pieces, brush with oil and sprinkle over the salt.

Place on an oven tray with the garlic cloves and roast for 15-20 minutes until soft.

Skin the garlic and place in a blender with the roasted pumpkin and harissa, blend until smooth, add a little vegetable stock if you prefer a thinner sauce.

To serve, place a square of polenta in the centre of each serving plate, cross over two parsnip halves on top and pour over the pumpkin sauce. Garnish with coriander leaves.

SERVES 4

BRUSCHETTA & DIPS

MARINATED POACHED
TOMATO BRUSCHETTA

GRILLED FIG
AND BASTOURMA
BRUSCHETTA

SPICY GLAZED ONION
AND GOATS CHEESE BRUSCHETTA

ANCHOVY AND
BOCCONCINI BRUSCHESTA

EGGPLANT BRUSCHETTA

2 tablespoons olive oil
1 teaspoon cumin seeds, crushed
2 cloves garlic, roughly chopped
1 medium eggplant (aubergine)
1 teaspoon fresh thyme
1 tablespoon lemon juice
Sea salt and cracked pepper, to taste
4 pieces of toasted bread, preferably ciabatta
1 tablespoon sesame seeds

Preheat the oven to moderate 180°C (350°F) Gas Mark 4.

In small bowl, combine half the olive oil, half the cumin and half the garlic.

Cut the eggplant in half and brush each half with the combined ingredients.

Place on an oven tray with the flesh side down and roast for about 10 minutes or until soft.

Take out the flesh from the skin and dice into small cubes.

Whisk together the rest of the oil, cumin and garlic with the thyme, lemon juice, salt and pepper.
Mix with the eggplant.

Place on top of the toasted bruschetta and sprinkle over the sesame seeds.

SERVES 4

SPICY GLAZED ONION
AND GOATS CHEESE BRUSCHETTA

1 tablespoon argan oil
1 medium brown onion, finely chopped
1 teaspoon *ras el hanout*
2 tablespoons apple cider
½ teaspoon chilli powder
1 tablespoon soft brown sugar
4 pieces of toasted bread, preferably ciabatta
125g (4oz) soft goats cheese

Heat the oil in a frying pan and sauté the onion until golden brown, being careful not to let it burn.

Throw in the *ras el hanout*, apple cider and chilli powder, stir and then mix in the sugar.

Cook on a low heat until thick and glazed.

Chill.

Place on top of the bruschetta, lay over slices of goats cheese and serve.

SERVES 4

MARINATED POACHED
TOMATO BRUSCHETTA

3 organic tomatoes
2 tablespoons argan oil
1 tablespoon white vinegar
Salt and white cracked pepper, to taste
6 fresh basil leaves, hand torn
½ Spanish onion, finely chopped
4 pieces of toasted bread, preferably ciabatta

Place tomatoes in enough boiling water to cover for 2 minutes. Drain. Cut a cross at the stem end and peel off the skin. De-seed and dice.

In a salad bowl, combine the oil, vinegar, salt, pepper, fresh basil and onion.

Serve on top of the toasted bruschetta.

SERVES 4

SEMI-DRIED TOMATO
AND SMOKED SALMON BRUSCHETTA

SEMI-DRIED TOMATO
AND SMOKED SALMON BRUSCHETTA

100g (3½oz) soft semi-dried tomatoes
1 tablespoon capers
2 tablespoons plain yoghurt
1 tablespoon zaatar
100g (3½oz) smoked salmon
4 pieces of toasted bread, preferably ciabatta
1 tablespoon finely sliced Spanish onion, sliced as thinly as possible
1 tablespoon argan oil
Salt and pepper, to taste

Chop up the semi-dried tomatoes and combine with the capers, yoghurt and zaatar in a small bowl.

Place the salmon on top of the bruschetta and top with the semi-dried tomato mix, garnish with the onion and drizzle over the argan oil. Season.

SERVES 4

GRILLED FIG AND
BASTOURMA BRUSCHETTA

GRILLED FIG AND
BASTOURMA BRUSCHETTA

2 medium ripe figs
1 tablespoon pomegranate molasses
4 slices *bastourma* (dry cured spicy beef)
4 pieces of toasted bread, preferably ciabatta
1 tablespoon *dukkah*

Marinate the figs in the pomegranate molasses for half an hour and cut into thick slices.

Lightly grill (broil) the slices on both sides.

Place the *bastourma* on each bruschetta, and top with the slices of grilled fig.

Sprinkle over the *dukkah* and serve.

SERVES 4

ROASTED RED AND
GREEN CAPSICUM BRUSCHETTA

1 red capsicum (bell pepper)
1 green capsicum
1 teaspoon coriander (cilantro) seeds
2 tablespoons argan oil
2 cloves garlic, crushed
1 tablespoon fresh coriander, chopped
1 tablespoon lemon juice
4 pieces of toasted bread, preferably ciabatta
Salt and cracked black pepper, to taste

Roast the capsicums on a hot chargrill or over a flame for a few minutes until blistered and blackened on all sides. Place in a plastic bag for a few minutes to sweat, then peel off the skin, halve, remove seeds and membrane and dice the flesh into small pieces.

Toast the coriander seeds in a frypan over a low heat until fragrant.

Crush the seeds in a mortar and pestle and add in the oil, garlic, fresh coriander and lemon juice, mix well then stir through the capsicum.

Serve on top of the toasted bruschetta and sprinkle with salt and pepper.

Enjoy while still warm so you can really taste the delicate flavours of the smoky capsicum and the argan oil.

SERVES 4

MIXED OLIVES
AND *HARISSA* BRUSCHETTA

MIXED OLIVES
AND HARISSA BRUSCHETTA

1 cup green, black and purple olives, pitted,
1 teaspoon *harissa*
1 tablespoon parsley
1 tablespoon coriander (cilantro)
1 tablespoon olive oil
1 tablespoon diced preserved lemon
½ cup ricotta cheese
4 pieces of toasted bread, preferably ciabatta
1 tablespoon fresh mint leaves

Halve the olives, place in a large bowl and mix with the *harissa*, parsley, coriander, olive oil and preserved lemon. Do not add any salt and pepper.

Spread the ricotta over the bruschetta and spoon on the olive mix.

Garnish with mint and serve.

SERVES 4

ANCHOVY AND BOCCONCINI BRUSCHETTA

ANCHOVY AND

BOCCONCINI BRUSCHETTA

1 tablespoon blue vein cheese
2 tablespoons warm water
4 tinned anchovies, finely chopped
100g (3½oz) bocconcini (about 4 medium balls)
½ avocado, sliced widthways in to 4 pieces
1 teaspoon olive oil
1 teaspoon chopped thyme
4 cherry tomatoes
4 pieces of toasted bread, preferably ciabatta

Mix the blue cheese in a small bowl with the warm water until creamy.

Add the anchovies and combine for a thick dressing.

Slice the bocconcini to the same thickness as the avocado.

Place one piece of avocado beside one piece of bocconcini on the bruschetta, slightly overlapping each other.

Drizzle with the dressing.

For the final touch, heat the olive oil and lightly fry the thyme and cherry tomatoes for 1 minute and place cherry tomato and thyme on each bruschetta.

SERVES 2

CARROT DIP

1kg (2lbs) carrots, washed, peeled and with the top removed
½ cup vegetable oil
4 cloves garlic, peeled and crushed
1 tablespoon cumin
1 teaspoon hot Hungarian paprika
1 teaspoon sweet paprika
1 cup flat leaf parsley
2 tablespoons vinegar
2 tablespoons icing sugar
Salt and pepper, to taste

Cut the carrots in half lengthways and cut out the core. Boil in salted water until soft, then dice.

Heat the oil in a large pan and fry the garlic and carrot for a few minutes before stirring through the spices. Cook until it becomes fragrant.

Add in the parsley then as it dries out pour in the vinegar. Remove from the heat.

It can now be eaten as is as a warm salad but to make the dip put the mixture through a food processor or blender until it becomes a smooth but thick puree.

Stir in the icing sugar and the salt and pepper and serve with warm bread.

MAKES 3 CUPS

BESARA GREEN PEA DIP

1 cup olive oil
8 cloves garlic, peeled and crushed
1 teaspoon cumin
500g (1lb) dried green peas
1½ litres (2½ pints) water
1 tablespoon olive oil
1 teaspoon sweet paprika

Heat the oil in a large pan and add the garlic to sizzle, then the cumin and dried peas and stir for a few minutes. Add in 1 litre (1¾ pints) of the water and boil for about 20 minutes, stirring often.

As it becomes drier gradually add in the remaining water.

Take off the heat and leave to stand for 15 minutes. At this point you can choose to put through a blender or leave it chunky as I do.

Put it back on the heat and cook until the peas split and soften, appoximatey 10 minutes. Stir in the harissa and cook for another 5 minutes, stirring constantly.

Allow to cool before serving with warm bread and garnishing with a swirl of olive oil and a sprinkle of paprika.

MAKES 4 CUPS

CARROT DIP

BESARA GREEN PEA DIP

BEETROT DIP

BEETROT DIP

BEETROOT DIP

BEETROT DIP

2 tablespoons olive oil
2 cloves garlic, crushed
1kg (2lbs) beetroot, peeled and cubed
2 medium carrots, peeled and with the tops cut off
1 teaspoon salt
1 teaspoon ground white pepper
1 cup orange juice
1 teaspoon sweet cinnamon powder
½ bunch fresh dill, chopped

Heat the oil and garlic in a large pan over medium heat, then add in the beetroot and carrots.

Stir in the salt and pepper, allowing it to sizzle before pouring in the orange juice. Simmer for 15 minutes then add in the cinnamon and dill, stir them through then remove from the heat and allow to cool.

Once cooled, place into a blender and blend until smooth.

Serve garnished with some fresh dill.

MAKES 5 CUPS

PRESERVED OLIVES

PRESEVED OLIVES
PRESEVED OLIVES

8kg (16lbs) fresh olives (preferably red varieties)
4kg (8lbs) oranges, juiced, keep skins
4kg (8lbs) lemons, juiced, keep skins
2kg (4lbs) rock salt
2 globes fennel

Break every olive by just hitting them with a rolling pin or by creating slits with a knife. Wash them with cold water in a big pot before transferring into a large drum big enough to fit all the olives, traditionally made of terracotta.

Cover with water and store in a cool place, changing the water 4 times in 10 days, almost every second day.

On the 10th day, instead of water, pour in the orange juice, lemon juice, lemon skins, salt and fennel then top up with water to ensure the olives are covered.

Either keep in the large drum or transfer to smaller jars or containers if you prefer. Seal tightly and leave somewhere cool like a wine cellar to preserve untouched for a minimum of 1 month. Olives should last for about 12 months once preserved.

TAJINES

SLOW COOKING

Tajine is the name for the cooking pot as well as the dish prepared in the pot. The traditional tajine is made entirely from clay, which is then glazed to give it a terracotta finish. There are two parts, the heavy, flat circular bottom with low sides and the conical, dome shaped lid which fits inside the bottom. Tajines vary in finish, some are highly decorative and European manufacturers are now making them from cast iron. Choice is great, but personally I prefer the rustic, original style because it is more robust and retains the earthy flavour that the tajine is famous for.

The tajine is designed for use over very low gas or a charcoal heat source to allow a long, slow cooking time and tender meat which falls off the bone while retaining a rustic flavour from the earthenware pot. The idea is that you place your ingredients inside, arranged as you would like them to look when serving to the table, place the lid on top, put it onto a low flame and leave it to cook. The pressure will build up inside the conical lid, cooking your dish from both the bottom and the top—just like a pressure cooker—perhaps it is an ancient example of one. The hollow knob on the top of the tajine lid serves two purposes; it allows you to easily remove the lid because generally it stays cool (but be careful, some can get very hot) and it was also used as a timer in early days, before the luxury of clocks and watches. Water was put into the knob and when this evaporated the tajine was ready. For longer cooking times, for example lamb dishes rather than fish, the knob would be filled more than once.

My aim in this book is to show that the tajine is easy to use and a delightful way to cook. You can blend exotic meats with fruit and vegetables and combine fresh local produce with herbs and spices to give your guests a taste sensation like no other. Tajines for breakfast, lunch and dinner—see how easy it is!

BREAKFAST TAJINES

VEGETABLE BREAKFAST TAJINE
VEGETABLE BREAKFAST TAJINE

VEGETABLE BREAKFAST TAJINE

1 tablespoon cumin seeds
½ eggplant (aubergine)
Salt, to taste
½ sweet potato, peeled and cut into 1cm (½in) cubes
¼ cup (60ml/2fl oz) olive oil
½ leek (white part only), sliced
½ cup fresh peas
1 tomato peeled, pitted and chopped
1 teaspoon *harissa*
8 baby English spinach (silverbeet) leaves
3 bocconcini, sliced
4 eggs, beaten
2 tablespoons fresh coriander (cilantro), chopped

Preheat oven to modrately hot 200°C (400F) Gas Mark 5.

In a pan, roast cumin seeds and crush.

Prepare eggplant by halving lengthways and sprinkle the flesh side with half of the salt and cumin. Slice 1cm (½in) thick lengthwise leaving the stalk intact. Place on a greased baking tray, flesh side down.

Coat sweet potato with the remaining cumin and place on the baking tray with the eggplant, drizzle both with a little of the olive oil and put in the oven to roast for approximately 20 minutes.

While these are cooking, in a medium tajine, heat remaining olive oil over low heat, fry the leek and peas until soft. Add diced tomatoes, *harissa* and cook for 5 minutes.

Take eggplant and sweet potato from the oven, slice cooked eggplant into cubes, discard the stalk and mix with the sweet potato. Add to the tajine and mix through. Sprinkle on leftover salt, lay spinach over and top with bocconcini, then pour eggs and coriander over the top. Place lid on tajine and cook for a further 5 minutes.

Serve while steaming hot.

SERVES 2

The best way to buy mussels is fresh and alive, although they are also sold cooked and preserved in either oil or sauce. When you're buying fresh they must be tightly closed or snap shut when tapped; this shows they're still alive and edible. You should cook them within three days of being caught.

SEAFOOD BREAKFAST TAJINE

SEAFOOD BREAKFAST TAJINE

SEAFOOD BREAKFAST TAJINE

4 green king prawns (shrimps)
1 tablespoon green peppercorns
1 clove garlic, smashed
8 green lip mussels (clams), brushed and cleaned
4 baby onions, peeled
1 tablespoon butter
6 fresh scallops
4 eggs, beaten
1 tablespoon capers
2 shallots (spring onions), chopped
4 semi-dried tomatoes

Peel prawns, leaving the heads on. In a pan of 2 cups of water, add prawns shells, green peppercorns and garlic and bring to the boil. Add mussels, cover the pan and cook for approximately 2 minutes, until mussels open.

Take out mussels and set aside.

Continue to boil stock until reduced by half, then strain into another pan.

Slice baby onions in half lengthways and add to stock, boil for a further 5 minutes.

In a tajine, melt the butter, add stock and onions, heat then arrange prawns, scallops and mussels, pour over eggs, add capers and cook for further 5 minutes.

Serve garnished with shallots and semi-dried tomatoes.

SERVES 2

MERGUEZ
CONCASSE BREAKFAST TAJINE

MERGUEZ
CONCASSE BREAKFAST TAJINE

1 tablespoon olive oil
300g (9½oz) *merguez* sausages
1 cup tomato *concasse*
½ cup black olives
4 eggs
1 tablespoon continental parsley, finely chopped

In a bowl, mix the olive oil with the sausages.

Place sausages onto a chargrill and cook for approximately 1 minute (they only need to be half cooked at this stage and the chargrill gives them a lovely smoky flavour).

Place a 2 person sized tajine over low heat, add tomato *concasse*, arrange sausages on top, sprinkle with olives and heat for 5 minutes.

Once the tomato is bubbly, make small wells in it and break in the eggs, place the lid on and leave until the eggs are poached to your liking (approximately 5 minutes).

Sprinkle with parsley and serve.

SERVES 2

MERGUEZ SAUSAGES

MERGUEZ SAUSAGES

MERGUEZ SAUSAGES

2 tablespoons *ras el hanout*
2 tablespoons *harissa*
1 tablespoon garlic, crushed
½ cup (125ml/4fl oz) tomato paste
1 tablespoon sweet paprika
1 bunch coriander (cilantro), chopped
1 preserved lemon, chopped
1 tablespoon olive oil
2kg (4lbs) minced (ground) beef or cubed beef (keep fat on)
Sausage skins

In a bowl, combine *ras el hanout*, *harissa*, garlic, tomato paste, paprika, coriander and preserved lemon. Mix well, then add olive oil and beef. Mix well again, making sure the meat is well coated with the spices.

Allow to stand for 1 hour.

Put the mixture through a mincer and then in to sausage skins. Make the sausages approximately 6cm (2½ins) long. Alternatively take the mixture to a butcher and get the sausages made up for you.

SERVES 4

TOMATO CONCASSÉ

TOMATO CONCASSÉ
TOMATO CONCASSÉ

1 tablespoon olive oil
2 garlic cloves, crushed
8 Roma tomatoes, peeled, seeded and diced
1 tablespoon butter, optional

Heat the olive oil in a saucepan over medium heat and add the garlic, cook for 30 seconds. Stir in the tomatoes and bring to the boil. Reduce the heat and simmer for about 10 minutes, until slightly reduced and thickened. Whisk in the butter, if using, until it is melted.

Concassé simply means 'coarsely chopped'. The tomatoes can be pureed in a food processor or blender for a smoother sauce, if you like.

CHEESE BREAKFAST TAJINE

CHEESE BREAKFAST TAJINE

CHEESE BREAKFAST TAJINE

1 cup *charmoula* sauce
1 cup oyster mushrooms
4 eggs, lightly whisked
Salt and pepper, to taste
100g (3½oz) gorgonzola
100g (3½oz) cheddar
120g (4oz) camembert
100g (3½oz) goats cheese
1 tablespoon chives, chopped

Heat a tajine over a low heat, line the bottom with *charmoula* sauce, arrange the mushrooms on top, then cook for 2 minutes until bubbling. Pour over the eggs, making sure to spread evenly. Season.

Shave gorgonzola and cheddar over the top to cover the eggs, arrange pieces of camembert and goats cheese on top of this, then place the lid on top and cook for 5 minutes until the cheeses are melted.

Sprinkle chives over the top and serve with crispy baguette or bread of your choice.

SERVES 2

MAIN COURSE TAJINES

Again, the best way to buy mussels is fresh and alive, although they are also sold cooked and preserved in either oil or sauce. When you're buying fresh they must be tightly closed or snap shut when tapped; this shows they're still alive and edible. You should cook them within three days of being caught.

TAJINE OF MUSSELS

TAJINE OF MUSSELS

TAJINE OF MUSSELS

1.5kg (3lbs) black or green mussels (clams)
1 tablespoon extra virgin olive oil
2 cloves garlic, crushed
1 leek, sliced
½ lemon, juiced
1 cup (250ml/8fl oz) dry white wine
1 thread saffron
Couple sprigs thyme
1 tablespoon blue vein cheese
1 bay leaf
1 teaspoon salt
1 teaspoon ground black pepper
400ml (13fl oz)1 tin coconut milk
1 cup tomato *concasse*
1 bunch chives or thyme, chopped

Mussels must be completely cleaned by removing anything attached to them. Brush and scrape the shells under cold running water. Pull the cluster of fine dark hairs away from the shell.

In a wide shallow pan with a tight lid, heat the oil and fry the garlic and leek. Add mussels, lemon juice and wine, cover and cook on high heat for 2 minutes. Remove the opened mussels with tongs and place them in a large tajine. Add the saffron, thyme, cheese, bay leaf, salt, pepper and coconut milk.

Allow this to reduce over low heat for about 10 minutes—it must not be too thick. Add tomato *concasse* and remove from heat. Pour the sauce over the layer of mussels in the tajine. Steam with lid on for 2 minutes.

Serve in soup bowls topped with chives.

SERVES 4

QUAIL AND GOATS CHEESE TAJINE WITH BRAISED PICKLED ONIONS AND RAISINS

8 large vine leaves
4 x 200g (6½oz) quail, de-boned
1 tablespoon *smen* (aged butter) or 1 tablespoon
    blue cheese melted in 1 tablespoon boiling water.
Salt and freshly ground black pepper, to taste
1 bunch spinach (silverbeet), stems removed
1 garlic clove, crushed
½ teaspoon grated nutmeg
¼ cup toasted pistachio nuts, chopped
1 teaspoon thyme
2 tablespoons fresh goats cheese
½ cup breadcrumbs
Salt and freshly ground black pepper, to taste
1 egg, beaten
50ml (2fl oz) olive oil
8 rashers *bastourma* (dry cured spicy beef)

Braised Pickled Onions
2 tablespoons olive oil
750g (1½lbs) small brown pickling onions
300ml (10fl oz) chicken stock
2 garlic cloves, chopped
2 bay leaves
350g (11oz) can tomatoes, diced
50g (2oz) dried cranberries
Saffron thread, pinch

Preheat oven to hot, 220°C (450°F) Gas Mark 6.

Wash and dry the vine leaves and set aside.

Using a paper towel, flatten and dry the quail thoroughly, then rub the *smen* or blue cheese mix onto the underside of the birds and season.

To prepare the stuffing, blanch the spinach leaves for 2 minutes in boiling salted water, drain in a colander and then refresh with cold water. Squeeze out all the moisture then roughly chop.

In a bowl, combine the spinach, garlic, nutmeg, pistachio nuts, thyme, goats cheese, and breadcrumbs and mix well. Add salt and pepper, pour in the egg and olive oil, then mix gently to combine all ingredients.

Distribute the stuffing evenly between the de-boned quail, making sure not to over fill. Using two vine leaves for each quail, wrap the birds and tuck the edges back under.

Wrap each one with two slices of *bastourma* and tie with cooking string, brush all over with the *smen* or blue cheese mix and then wrap each bird tightly in foil.

Place the quail in a roasting dish and bake for 15 minutes or roast on a spit for 10 minutes.

To prepare the braised pickled onions, heat the olive oil in a pan and sauté the onions until brown, being careful not to burn.

Add half the stock and boil until evaporated, then add garlic, bay leaves, tomatoes, cranberries, saffron and the remaining stock and bring to boil. Turn down the heat and cover the pan and simmer for 20 minutes.

Transfer the sauce to the tajine.

Remove the string from the wrapped quail and place the birds in the centre of the sauce and pickled onions in the tajine and cook for a further 10 minutes. Serve hot.

SERVES 4

This simple, quick and tasty recipe reminds me of Essaouirra, the white city on the Atlantic coast of Morocco with its historical old medina. I love to stroll along the old port enjoying the strong smell of smoke from the fresh sardines on the market grill mixing with the fresh sea salt. The town's signature tajines steam away in the lines of restaurants, one beside the other nestled in the valley. Visitors and locals alike enjoy choosing their fish and taking their bucket to the grills to be cleaned and cooked—all part of a wonderful seafood town experience.

SARDINE AND PERCH KEFTA TAJINE

SARDINE AND PERCH KEFTA TAJINE

SARDINE AND PERCH KEFTA TAJINE

500g (1lb) sardine fillets
500g (1lb) perch fillets
1 bunch parsley
1 bunch coriander
1 teaspoon cumin seeds, roasted and crushed
1 teaspoon paprika
3 cloves garlic, crushed
1 tablespoon olive oil
Salt and pepper, to taste

Tajine base
¼ cup (60ml/2fl oz) olive oil
2 cloves garlic, crushed
Salt and pepper, to taste
3 organic tomatoes, sliced
½ preserved lemon, sliced and diced
1 cup fish stock

To prepare the kefta in the traditional way, dice the sardine and perch fillets into very small pieces and mix with parsley, coriander, cumin seeds, paprika, garlic, olive oil, salt and pepper.

Mince the ingredients with your hands—really feel it.

Alternatively, you can mix the same ingredients together in a bowl and put them through a mincer.

Wet your hands and roll the mince into walnut sized balls and place onto a tray about 1cm (½in) apart, while you prepare the tajine.

Place the tajine over a low heat, add oil, garlic, salt and pepper and stir until the garlic sizzles. Lay out the tomato to cover the base of the tajine then add the preserved lemon. Pour in the fish stock, simmer and stir for about 10 minutes.

Now gently add in the kefta balls, cover and leave to cook on the same heat for 15 minutes.

Serve hot, with a fresh salad and warm bread.

SERVES 4

Confit is one of the oldest forms of preserving food and is a specialty in the south-west of France. Meat is salted and slowly cooked in its own fat then placed in a pot and covered completely in a layer of fat to seal the pot and preserve the meat. The first time I tried this dish was on a visit to Carcassonne, Castelnaudary in France. It reminded me of klu, Moroccan preserved meat, and the way it's cooked in a special earthenware pot.

CASSOULET TAJINE

CASSOULET TAJINE

CASSOULET TAJINE

3 cups white haricot beans
4 confit leg of goose or turkey
2 stalks thyme
¼ cup olive oil
½ tablespoon freshly ground pepper
½ tablespoon salt
600g (1lb3oz) lamb shoulder, cut in quarters
500g (1lb) good fat sausage
2 onions, chopped
4 garlic cloves, crushed
4 tomatoes, peeled, seeded (pitted) and crushed
1 cup breadcrumbs
1 bunch coriander, chopped

Soak the beans overnight in cold water. Do not use warm water as they may ferment and produce poisonous substances.

In a large pan, melt the fat off the confit and reserve the fat.

Heat the oil, rub salt, pepper and thyme in to the lamb and fry until brown. When cooked through add the sausage and half cook.

Remove all the meat from the bones and keep aside.

Preheat oven to moderately slow, 160°C (325°F) Gas Mark 3.

Fry onion and garlic in the meat fat, add crushed tomatoes,

Drain the beans and add to the sauce. Stir in enough water to cover the beans well. Simmer gently for 45 minutes so that the beans remain intact.

Cut meat into equal pieces and the sausage into slices or small circles.

Place a layer of beans in the tajine, then a layer of meat and sauce, then another layer of beans, seasoning as you go with pepper.

Sprinkle breadcrumbs and the reserved melted fat over the top.

Cook gently in the oven for about 1½ hours until a brown crust forms on top. Garnish with coriander and serve hot in the tajine—that's when it's really tasty.

SERVES 4

This is not a particularly sweet dish but rather a combination of sweet spices. Inhale the exotic perfumes of cinnamon, nutmeg, saffron and orange blossom and enjoy the light but interesting flavours.

RABBIT TAJINE WITH

RABBIT TAJINE WITH
SAFFRON AND CHICKPEAS

SAFFRON AND CHICKPEAS

½ teaspoon saffron threads
2 cloves garlic, crushed
1 lemon, juiced
1/3 cup (80ml/21/fl oz) honey
1 teaspoon salt
1 tablespoon thyme leaves, chopped
¼ teaspoon ground nutmeg
1.8kg (3½lbs) farmed white rabbit
— ask your butcher to remove the front and hind legs and cut the saddle in half widthways
2 tablespoons olive oil
3 brown onions, sliced
2 bay leaves
2 tablespoons roughly chopped coriander (cilantro)
500ml (16fl oz) chicken stock
400g (13oz) chickpeas, soaked over night, peeled and split
¾ cup raisins
60ml (2fl oz) orange blossom water
¼ teaspoon ground cinnamon
1 tablespoon cracked white pepper

In a large bowl, combine the saffron, garlic, lemon juice, honey, salt, thyme, and nutmeg.

Marinate the rabbit pieces in the mixture and refrigerate for 1 hour.

Heat the oil on high in a large flame dish until very hot, reduce to medium heat and fry the rabbit pieces, browning both sides. Using a slotted spoon take out the rabbit pieces and leave aside on a plate. Cover with foil.

In the same pan, cook the onion and marinade mixture until the onion is soft.

Stir in the bay leaves before adding the rabbit, coriander, stock and chickpeas.

Cover and leave to cook for about 40 minutes, adding more water if necessary.

Soak the raisins in the orange blossom water for 30 minutes.

Transfer the rabbit pieces to a large tajine suitable for about 4 people.

Add the raisins, cinnamon and white peppers to the chickpea sauce and stir.

Pour the sauce and chickpeas over the rabbit and cook in the tajine over a low heat for a further 10 minutes.

Serve hot with Moroccan bread.

SERVES 4

CHICKEN TAJINE

CHICKEN TAJINE
WITH FIGS AND WALNUTS

WITH FIGS AND WALNUTS

1kg (2lbs) fresh figs
1 teaspoon sweet cinnamon powder
½ teaspoon ginger powder
½ teaspoon nutmeg, ground
1 tablespoon water
2 tablespoons olive oil
2 salad onions, diced
2 cloves garlic, crushed
1 teaspoon ginger
Saffron threads, pinch, soaked in a little hot water to soften
Salt and pepper, to taste
1.4kg (2¾lbs) chicken, cut into 6 pieces
100g (3½oz) sweet red grapes (seedless)
¼ cup (60ml/2fl oz) honey
100g (3½oz) walnuts, chopped

Wash and dry the figs and cut them in half.

Combine the cinnamon, ginger, nutmeg and water in a bowl and mix well. Add the figs, mix gently and leave in a cool place for 1 hour.

Heat the oil in a large tajine, add the onion and garlic and gently cook until soft. Throw in the ginger, saffron threads, salt and pepper and the chicken pieces and cook for 5 minutes.

Add water to cover the bottom of the tajine and cook over low heat for approximately 45 minutes, turning the chicken occasionally.

Garnish with the marinated figs and the grapes. Drizzle with honey and sprinkle with walnuts, replace the lid and cook for a further 10 minutes. Serve in the tajine.

SERVES 4

DOUARA
TRIPE, HEART AND
LIVER COUNTRY STYLE TAJINE

400g (13oz) sheep's tripe
1 litre (1¾ pints) beef stock
¼ cup (60ml/2fl oz) vinegar
½ teaspoon *harissa*
½ cup (125ml/4fl oz) olive oil
1 sheep heart, cubed
1 sheep liver, cubed
1 brown onion, thinly sliced
3 garlic cloves, chopped
200g (6½oz) carrots, diced 1cm (½in) thick
2 tomatoes, pitted and chopped
1 teaspoon sweet red paprika
½ teaspoon cumin powder
Salt and fresh ground black pepper, to taste
150g (5oz) shallots (spring onions), finely chopped

Bouquet garni
1 tablespoon fresh thyme leaves
¼ cup fresh parsley leaves
1 tablespoon lemon zest
3 bay leaves

Place the bouquet garni ingredients into a clean square of cheesecloth or similar, wrap at the top and tie with string.

Clean and cut the tripe into 1cm x 10cm (½in x 4in) strips. Put into a heavy based stockpot or crockpot and cover with the beef stock, add the bouquet garni and bring to the boil, reduce heat to simmer for approximately 12 hours or until the tripe is soft.

In a bowl, make a marinade by mixing together the vinegar, *harissa* and ½ of the olive oil. Add the heart and liver cubes, mix together and refrigerate for 1 hour.

Remove the tripe from the stock and strain off any liquid, remove the bouquet garni and set aside. Bring the stock to the boil and reduce by half.

Heat the remaining olive oil in a large tajine over medium heat, add the onion and garlic and cook until soft.

Add the carrots, tomatoes, paprika, cumin, salt and pepper and stir together.

Then add the marinated heart and liver, place the tripe on top, then pour over the reduced stock.

Place the lid on the tajine and reduce the heat to low and simmer for 30 minutes until all the meat and vegetables are tender.

Take off the heat and sprinkle the shallots on top, serve in the tajine with the lid on—removing the lid when ready to serve.

SERVES 4

DUCK TAJINE WITH CUMQUAT
CONFIT AND GLAZED TURNIP

DUCK TAJINE WITH CUMQUAT
CONFIT AND GLAZED TURNIP

4 duck legs, approximately 180g (2½oz) each
1 tablespoon salt
½ bunch thyme
1 large turnip, peeled and stalk removed
¼ cup (60ml/2fl oz) olive oil
1 tablespoon *smen* (aged butter) or blue cheese
50g (2oz) butter
2 onions, sliced
1 teaspoon nutmeg
1 saffron thread
Salt and pepper, to taste
½ cup caster sugar
250g (8oz) cumquats
2 cups (500ml/16fl oz) chicken stock
1 cup (250ml/8fl oz) fresh orange juice
2 teaspoons cider vinegar
1 tablespoon orange blossom water
1½ teaspoons sweet cinnamon
1 tablespoon sesame seeds, toasted

Season the duck legs with salt and thyme, seal with cling wrap then refrigerate for 4–5 hours.

Cut the turnip into segments. Boil in salted water for 1 minute then drain. Set aside.

Remove the duck legs from the salt mixture, rinse under cold running water and dry with a clean tea towel.

In a large saucepan, heat olive oil and *smen*, then add the duck legs, cover, and cook on all sides over low heat for 15 minutes, this will melt the fat. Remove excess fat from the pan and keep it in reserve.

Add butter, onions, nutmeg, saffron, salt, pepper and 2 tablespoons of the sugar to the pan of duck legs, stir and sizzle on very low heat for 10 minutes.

Wash the cumquats, split them in half then add to pan and stir with ⅓ cup of the sugar. Pour in chicken stock and orange juice and cook, uncovered, stirring occasionally until reduced to a soft compote of an even consistency.

Scatter over the remaining ¼ cup of caster sugar and sauté until it begins to caramelise. Add cider vinegar, orange blossom water and 1 teaspoon of the cinnamon. Transfer to a baking dish and set aside.

Heat the reserved duck fat in a frying pan until very hot, then add the turnips and toss to coat them with the fat.

Place the duck pieces in the middle of a large tajine for 4–6 people, cover with the cumquat and onion compote and arrange the glazed turnips in a dome shape all around the duck pieces.

Finally, sprinkle the whole dish with the remaining sweet cinnamon, cover and heat for 5 more minutes. Sprinkle with toasted sesame seeds. Serve hot.

SERVES 4

The yellow-skinned quince looks and tastes like a cross between an apple and a pear and has been popular as far back as the ancient Greeks and Romans. I think the flavour of quince goes very well with poultry.

CHICKEN TAJINE WITH QUINCE

CHICKEN TAJINE WITH QUINCE

CHICKEN TAJINE WITH QUINCE

1.6kg (3¼lbs) chicken, cut in to 8 pieces
2 tablespoons fresh mint leaves
2 teaspoons saffron thread
½ teaspoon yellow food colouring powder
1 cup (250ml/8fl oz) orange juice
Salt and freshly ground black pepper, to taste
100g (3½oz) butter
2 tablespoons olive oil
2 brown onions, julienned
2 teaspoons powdered ginger
1 stick sweet cinnamon
3 cups water
2 ripe quinces, cords and seeds removed, cut into 8 pieces
¼ cup (60ml/2fl oz) honey
1 teaspoon ground sweet cinnamon
500g (1lb) minted fresh broad beans

Wash and dry the chicken.

In a large bowl, mix together the mint, saffron and yellow colour, orange juice and season with salt and pepper. Toss the chicken into this mixture and marinate for at least 1 hour.

Heat the butter and olive oil in a large pot, add the onions and cook until soft, add the ginger and cinnamon stick then the marinated chicken, add 2 cups of the water, place a lid on the pot and cook over a low heat for 30 minutes. Take out the chicken pieces and put into the base of a tajine.

Keep the stock on the heat and add in the quince pieces, the honey, cinnamon and remaining 1 cup water, stir gently and bring to the boil, then reduce to a simmer, cover the pot and cook for 15 minutes.

Pour the quince sauce over the chicken in the tajine add the broad beans, place over a low gas heat and simmer for 10 minutes. Serve with steamed couscous or crusty bread.

SERVES 4

COUSCOUS

HAPPINESS & ABUNDANCE

As Germany has schnitzel, Italy has pasta and France has baguettes and croissants, so Morocco has couscous, the traditional Berber dish that usually accompanies a stew of meat and vegetables. It is the epitome of Moroccan cuisine, appreciated the world over and, according to one culinary anthropologist, its preparation symbolises 'happiness and abundance'.

Cooking couscous is a hugely important part of Moroccan culture, essential at weddings and funerals and given in charity to poor or sick people in the neighbourhood in order to bring blessings on the entire family.

Couscous is the name of the dish and also the process by which this rice or pasta type food is prepared. It is made by rolling and shaping moistened semolina wheat and then coating it with finely ground wheat flour. Enjoy couscous with friends and family as part of a meal for a real taste of Morocco.

If you want to make the best couscous, cooked the way they do it in Morocco, it's a good idea to invest in a *couscousier*, a large aluminium, brass or stainless steel pot with a tight fitting colander with fine holes and a lid.

FOR SWEET DISHES

4 litres (7 pints) water
1 tablespoon salt
3 bay leaves
½ teaspoon black peppercorns
2 cinnamon sticks
Pinch saffron threads
500g (1lb) couscous
100g (3½oz) butter

Pour 3 litres (4¾ pints) of water in the bottom of the *couscousier*, add half the salt, the bay leaves, peppercorns and cinnamon sticks and bring to the boil.

In a saucepan, add the other 1 litre (1¾ pints) of water with the saffron and remaining salt and heat until almost at boiling point.

Put the couscous into a shallow bowl and cover with half the saffron water, allow to soak up the liquid for 10 minutes, whilst stirring gently with a wooden spoon. Then, using your fingers, separate the grains and rub out all lumps (doing this at the beginning prevents lumpy couscous later).

Place glad wrap or cheesecloth around the lip of the bottom part of the *couscousier*, place the top part on (this process prevents any steam escaping—allowing it to steam through the couscous).

Put the couscous into the top part of the *couscousier*, spreading evenly, wait until the stream starts to come through the grain (make sure there is no steam escaping out between the two pots) and allow to steam for 5 minutes.

Take out the couscous, return to the bowl once more, add the remaining saffron water, fluff up and remove any lumps with your fingers again. Leave to sit for 10 minutes before placing back into the *couscousier* and steaming for another 5 minutes.

Take out the couscous and return to the bowl once more, add the remaining saffron water, fluff up and remove any lumps with your fingers, add the butter and mix through with your fingers (butter or oil is always added after the last steaming as this seals the grain).

Couscous can be kept refrigerated for up to 1 week and can be used hot or cold.

FOR SAVOURY DISHES

Follow the same steaming process as for sweet dishes but the stock in the bottom of the pot will change to savoury. Use vegetable, meat or fish stock, such as one made from fish heads, prawn heads and shells, with bay leaves, peppercorns, onion and garlic. There are numerous combinations of flavours and not a lot of limitations—experiment with your favourite stocks.

Instead of using butter to seal the grain, use extra virgin oil or smen.

The eggplant timbales need overnight refrigeration so be sure to make them one day ahead.

BAKED EGGPLANT TIMBALE WITH COUSCOUS, CRABMEAT AND MASCARPONE TAPENADE AND ROAST CAPSICUM AND TOMATO SAUCE

5 medium eggplants (aubergines)
Salt and cracked pepper, to taste
1 cup (250ml/8fl oz) extra virgin olive oil
2 cloves garlic, crushed
200g (6½oz) steamed couscous
½ bunch parsley
200g (6½oz) cooked crab meat
200g (6½oz) *mascarpone*
2 tablespoons black olive tapenade
1 tablespoon prepared saffron liquid

Sauce
6 medium ripe tomatoes
1 capsicum (bell pepper)
¼ cup (60ml/2fl oz) extra virgin olive oil
1 red onion, finely chopped
3 cloves garlic, chopped
100ml (3fl oz) white vinegar
Salt and pepper, to taste
1 tablespoon brown sugar
½ cup basil leaves
70g (2oz) blue cheese
125ml (4fl oz) buttermilk

Preheat the oven to moderate, 180°C (350°F) Gas Mark 4.

Take 1 of the eggplants, halve and rub with salt and pepper, brush with some olive oil and roast for 10 minutes or until soft. Turn off the heat and leave in the oven for another 5 minutes.

Peel off the skin or scoop out the flesh in one piece, then dice the flesh into small cubes.

Cut the ends off the remaining eggplants and slice in to ½cm (¼in) thick slices lengthways. Rub with salt and leave for a minute to remove any bitterness. Rinse off salt and pat dry.

Brush with olive oil and grill (broil) in a large pan on a high heat for about 2 minutes on each side or until cooked through and golden. Leave on paper towels to drain and allow to cool.

Fry the garlic with ¼ cup of olive oil in a saucepan. Add in the steamed couscous, parsley and crab meat, stir and turn off the heat.

In a small bowl, mix the mascarpone with the olive tapenade and saffron until combined.

Combine the mascarpone mix, couscous, crab meat and diced eggplant until well combined.

Line either a large muffin tray or 6 cup-sized moulds with plastic wrap, then line with the grilled eggplant slices, overlapping slightly.

Spoon in the mixture and press to firm. Fold the eggplant over the couscous and cover with the edges of the plastic.

Refrigerate overnight.

The next day, preheat the oven to slow, 140°C (300°F) Gas Mark 2.

Remove the plastic from the timbale and place on a baking paper lined tray, flat side down. Brush gently with oil and bake for 20 minutes or until cooked through.

To make the sauce, roast the capsicum on a hot chargrill or over a flame for a few minutes until it blisters and blackens on all sides. Place in a plastic bag for a few minutes to sweat, then peel off the skin, halve, remove seeds and membrane and dice the flesh into small pieces.

Plunge tomatoes in boiling water for 1–2 minutes and drain (this way the tomatoes remain raw and fresh with flavour). Peel off the skin, squeeze out the seeds and dice the flesh.

In a medium saucepan, heat the oil and fry the onion and garlic, add the tomato and capsicum and sizzle for 5 minutes.

Add the vinegar and simmer for 15 minutes, adding salt and pepper to taste and the brown sugar.

Turn off the heat, allow to cool slightly and then add the basil (leaving aside a few leaves for garnish) and puree in a blender.

In another saucepan over a low heat, crumble the blue cheese over a low heat in to the buttermilk, creaming it as you stir.

Pour in the capsicum and tomato sauce and cook for another 5 minutes, adding more salt and pepper if necessary.

Spoon sauce onto the centre of each serving plate. Place the eggplant timbale on top and garnish with fresh basil leaves. Serve hot.

SERVES 6

VINE LEAF AND COUSCOUS
WRAPPED SALMON FILO

WRAPPED SALMON FILO

8 medium–large fresh vine leaves
   (if not possible, preserved leaves will do)
8 sheets filo pastry
100g (3½oz) melted butter
250g (8oz) steamed couscous
2 fresh tomatoes, chopped into small pieces
2 teaspoons *harissa*
2 tablespoons chopped coriander (cilantro)
½ cup olive oil
4 x 150g (5oz) pieces salmon, filleted, skinned
   and de-boned (ideally cut to pieces 12cm x 5cm)
400g (13oz) baby spinach (silverbeet) leaves
1 tablespoon pearl caviar

Dressing
½ preserved lemon
1 clove garlic, crushed
¼ cup (60ml/2fl oz) olive oil
4 anchovies (tinned)
100g (3½oz) semi-dried tomatoes
Salt and pepper, to taste

Combine all dressing ingredients in a blender.

Preheat the oven to moderately slow, 160°C (325°F) Gas Mark 3.

Remove any thick stalks from the vine leaves. Rinse under cold water and boil in salted water for 3–4 minutes or until they become an olive green colour and tender.

Drain and run the leaves under ice-cold water, drain and dry on a paper towel.

Lay out 4 sheets of the filo pastry and brush them with butter and then lay another sheet on top of each and brush with butter too.

Place two vine leaves on each, covering the pastry as much as possible.

In a bowl, combine the couscous with the tomato, *harissa* and coriander along with 2 tablespoons of the olive oil.

Spread the couscous over the vine leaves.

Place a piece of the salmon lengthways on top of the couscous and roll up the pastry like a sushi roll.

Fold the ends like an envelope and brush the pastry with a mix of the remaining olive oil and a little of the remaining butter.

Pan fry the filo rolls lightly to seal the edges then place on an oven tray and bake for 10 minutes.

Melt the remaining butter in a pan and toss through the spinach, stirring until it has just lightly wilted.

Divide the spinach between each serving plate, top with a filo roll cut diagonally in half with the halves leaning on each other, drizzle over the dressing and garnish with a teaspoon of caviar. Enjoy.

SERVES 4

HARISSA

THE TRADITIONAL WAY TO MAKE HARISSA IS
WITH A MORTAR AND PESTLE BUT I PREFER
TO MAKE MINE WITH A MINCER THEN MIX
THOROUGHLY WITH A SPOON—THIS WAY I GET
THE COARSE TEXTURE I LIKE. IF YOU PREFER
A SMOOTH PASTE YOU CAN JUST PUT ALL
INGREDIENTS THROUGH A FOOD PROCESSOR.

GREEN *HARISSA*

GREEN *HARISSA*
GREEN *HARISSA*

1 preserved lemon
250g (8oz) small hot green chillies, stalks removed
1 bunch coriander (cilantro), including stalks, chopped
1 teaspoon sea salt
3 cloves of garlic
½ cup fresh mint leaves, chopped
1 tablespoon coriander seeds, toasted and crushed
1 cup olive oil

Chop up the preserved lemon and chillies and grind with the coriander stalks. Then add in the salt, garlic, mint, coriander leaves and seeds, all the while pouring in the olive oil and combining.

With all methods, once you've reached your desired consistency, set aside for an hour for the flavours to infuse.

Transfer to a glass jar with a tight lid. Can be stored indefinitely in the refrigerator.

MAKES 500ML (16FL OZ)

RED *HARISSA*

RED *HARISSA*
RED *HARISSA*

500g (1lb) small hot red chillies, stalks removed
2 large red capsicums (bell peppers),
 roasted and peeled
1 preserved lemon
3 garlic cloves
½ bunch coriander (cilantro), chopped
2 tablespoons ground cumin
1 tablespoon salt
Olive oil, to cover

Mince the chillies, roast capsicums (bell peppers), preserved lemon and garlic by hand or in a food processor. Mix with the coriander, cumin and salt until well combined. Let the mixture stand for 1 hour, then transfer to a preserving jar and cover with oil. Store indefinitely in the refrigerator.

MAKES ABOUT 4 CUPS

HARISSA AND MINTED

HARISSA AND MINTED
YOGHURT BAKED CHICKEN
WITH SWEET POTATO

WITH SWEET POTATO

1 tablespoon harissa
½ tablespoon ground cumin
½ cup mint leaves, chopped
Salt, to taste
1kg (2lbs) chicken thigh fillet
1 cup plain yoghurt
1kg (2lbs) sweet potato (kumara) peeled and diced
2 tablespoons argan oil
½ teaspoon ground nutmeg
1 teaspoon salt
100g (3½oz) mixed lettuce leaves
2 tablespoons lemon juice
1 tablespoon olive oil
4 mint leaves

In a bowl mix together the harissa, cumin, mint and salt, cover the chicken in this mix then coat in the yoghurt and leave in the fridge to marinade for 1 hour.

Preheat the oven to moderately hot, 200°C (400°F) Gas Mark 5.

Place chicken on a rack or on skewers in a baking dish and bake for 30 minutes or until cooked through and crispy.

Place the sweet potato in a baking dish, coat with argan oil and sprinkle with nutmeg and sea salt.

Bake for 20 minutes or until soft and golden.

Drizzle the leaves with lemon juice and oil, garnish with fresh mint leaves.

Serve chicken and potato hot with the salad.

SERVES 4

SARDINES STUFFED WITH *HARISSA*
WRAPPED IN VINE LEAVES

SARDINES STUFFED WITH *HARISSA* WRAPPED IN VINE LEAVES

16 preserved vine leaves
16 whole sardines, cleaned and boned
½ cup *harissa*
Olive oil
½ cup (125ml/4fl oz) minted *labneh*
4 lemon wedges, to serve

Carefully unfold the vine leaves and discard any brine.

Separate leaves and place in a large bowl, cover with boiling water and stand for 15 minutes.

Drain well then cover with cold water and stand for another 15 minutes.

Drain again on absorbent paper.

Place vine leaf flat on a work surface, then place a sardine across the centre of the leaf and place about ½ a teaspoon of *harissa* inside the body.

Carefully roll up the vine leaf around the sardine.

Repeat with the remaining sardines then brush them all with olive oil—this not only maintains the juices and flavour but also protects the sardines delicate flesh while cooking.

Heat the oil and cook the wrapped sardines in batches in a large heavy frypan for about 3 minutes on each side over a medium heat until cooked through.

Serve straight away on a flat dish, drizzle with *labneh* to calm the fiery spices for those who aren't quite used to the heat and serve with a fresh lemon wedge.

SERVES 4

WHOLE BAKED *DUKKAH*
AND GREEN *HARISSA*

WHOLE BAKED *DUKKAH* BARRAMUNDI WITH RED AND GREEN *HARISSA*

1 large whole barramundi, cleaned and scaled (about 2kg)
1 teaspoon sea salt
1 tablespoon freshly ground white pepper
100g (3½oz) whole raw almonds
½ preserved lemon
2 tablespoons extra virgin olive oil
2 cloves of garlic, crushed
1 red onion, peeled and chopped
½ bunch coriander (cilantro), finely chopped
2 tablespoons *dukkah*
1 cup natural yoghurt
1 tablespoon sesame seeds

Preheat the oven to moderate 180°C (350°F) Gas Mark 4.

Peel off and discard the topside of the barramundi skin, season with half of the salt and pepper, wrap in baking paper and keep aside.

Roast the almonds under a hot grill for 7 minutes or until browned and chop roughly.

Chop up the preserved lemon and whisk in a bowl with the olive oil, garlic, onion, coriander, *dukkah* and the rest of the salt and pepper.

Continue whisking as you add in the chopped almonds and the natural yoghurt to create a thick paste.

Spread the paste over the exposed barramundi flesh and cover with baking paper.

Place the wrapped fish on an oven tray and bake for about 30 minutes or until cooked through.

Serve on a large serving plate. Sprinkle with sesame seeds and accompany with red and green *harissa* and the lovely OOA salad.

SERVES 4

SPICES
ZAATAR, DUKKAH & RAS EL HANOUT

RAS EL
HANOUT

DUKKAH

ZAATAR

In North Africa, Jordan, Greece and Turkey this versatile spice mix is sprinkled onto food as a seasoning, used in recipes as a spice or served with bread and olive oil as a breakfast dish. You can buy ready mixed zaatar or you can make your own with this simple recipe. If stored well zaatar can last for up to 3 months.

ZAATAR ZAATAR

ZAATAR

2 tablespoons sesame seeds
1 tablespoon dried thyme
2 tablespoons dried oregano
1 tablespoon ground *sumac*

Dry roast the sesame seeds over a gentle heat in a fry pan until they are just coloured. Cool then grind them with the other herbs to a fine powder in a mortar and pestle. Store in a sealed jar.

MAKES ½ CUP

Dukkah is best served simply with some extra virgin olive oil and crusty bread. Keep it stored in an airtight container at room temperature.

DUKKAH DUKKAH

DUKKAH

50g (1¾oz) coriander seeds
50g (1¾oz) cumin seeds
100g (3⅓oz) sesame seeds
80g (2⅔oz) roasted hazelnuts
80g (2⅔oz) roasted almonds
30g (1oz) pink salt flakes
30g (1oz) ground black pepper

Toast the coriander and cumin seeds in a frying pan over medium heat, stirring often for about 1-2 minutes or until seeds start to pop and become aromatic. Place seeds in a mortar and pestle and crush to a coarse consistency.

Also over a medium heat, toast the sesame seeds, stirring, for 1-2 minutes or until a golden colour.

Crush the roasted nuts, being careful not to reduce them to a powder.

Mix them with the cumin and coriander, sesame seeds, salt and pepper in a bowl.

MAKES 400G (13OZ)

Ras el Hanout, which translates literally as 'Head of the Shop', originated in the Meghribi villages of North Africa. It is a complex and distinctive mix of about 20–27 spices and herbs, the quantities of which vary according to the maker. Specific quantities are a much guarded secret from one spice shop to the next, and blending is considered an art. Ras el Hanout is used with poultry, meat, game, rice and couscous. It can be found already mixed eg. in specialty stores. If you are unable to find it, here is a simple recipe for you to make your own.

RAS EL HANOUT

1½ teaspoons black peppercorns
1 teaspoon ground ginger
1 teaspoon cumin seeds
1 teaspoon coriander seeds
1 teaspoon ground cinnamon
¼ teaspoon ground nutmeg

¼ teaspoon cardamom seeds
¼ teaspoon hot paprika
4 whole cloves
¼ teaspoon ground turmeric
¼ teaspoon sea salt
¼ teaspoon ground allspice

Grind all the ingredients together with a mortar and pestle. Use as instructed in recipes.

MAKES ABOUT 2 TABLESPOONS

MINTED LABNEH WITH *ZAATAR*

2 cups (500g/1lb) natural yoghurt.
½ tablespoon salt
2 garlic cloves, crushed
2 tablespoons finely chopped mint
1 tablespoon lemon juice
¼ teaspoon *zaatar*

Combine the yoghurt and salt, then place into a muslin-lined sieve over a bowl, cover and refrigerate for at least 2 hours.

Discard liquid from yoghurt, do not squeeze.

Place into bowl, and stir through the remaining ingredients. Sprinkle with *zaatar*.

Serve as dipping sauce or dressing.

MAKES 500ML (16FL OZ)

I love brown lentils because they retain their shape and become tender rather than mushy when you cook them. They also readily absorb flavours and that is why I have chosen them for this dish which is rich in flavour and mixes delicate Moroccan ras el hanout and coconut.

FRESH SCALLOPS AND SALMON WITH CREAMY BROWN LENTILS

150g (5oz) brown lentils
2 cloves garlic, chopped
2 bay leaves
Salt, to taste
2 tablespoons olive oil
2 leeks, finely chopped (white part only)
1 saffron thread
100g (3½oz) sweet potato, diced small
2 teaspoons *ras el hanout*
150ml (5fl oz) fish stock
250ml (8fl oz) coconut milk
½ cup celery leaves, chopped
150ml (5fl oz) water
1kg (2lbs) fresh scallops
½kg (1lb) fresh salmon fillets, cut into thick slices (sushi style)
2 tablespoons chopped coriander (cilantro), to garnish

Place lentils in a large saucepan with one half of a garlic clove, bay leaves and salt, cover with cold water, bring to the boil, then simmer over medium heat for 10 minutes. Drain and set aside. To make the sauce, heat olive oil in a large, deep tajine (or a Berber tajine) and add the remaining garlic, leeks, saffron, sweet potatoes and *ras el hanout*. Cook stirring gently for 2 minutes, add fish stock and continue cooking until there is only half the liquid left. Add coconut milk, celery leaves and the lentils and water if needed. Bring to boil and stir well. Add the scallops and salmon, cover the tajine, reduce the heat and steam or simmer for 5 minutes.

Place scallops and salmon on top, cover tajine, reduce heat and simmer for 5 minutes.

Garnish with chopped coriander and serve.

SERVES 4

Baba literally translated means father and ghanouj means spoiled. Baba ghanouj or 'poor man's caviar' as it is also known, is a smoky paste made from the flesh of roasted eggplants.

BARBECUED BABY SQUID WITH BABA GHANOUJ AND HERB SALAD

Baba Ghanouj
1 large cooked eggplant (aubergine), roasted, grilled or smoked
120g (4oz) walnuts, soaked overnight in cold water
¼ cup mint leaves
1 clove of garlic, finely chopped
1 lemon, juiced
60ml (2fl oz) extra virgin olive oil
Salt and black pepper, to taste

6 whole baby squid
¹/₃ cup (80ml/2½fl oz) lemon juice
1 clove of garlic, crushed
¼ cup (60ml/2fl oz) olive oil
2 tablespoons *dukkah*
1 punnet coriander (cilantro) cress, trimmed and chopped
1 punnet chard cress, trimmed and chopped
1 punnet baby mache, trimmed and chopped
2 tablespoons *dukkah* dressing

To make the *baba ghanouj*, chop up the eggplant and place in a food processor with the walnuts, mint, garlic, lemon juice and process until blended. With the motor still running add the oil and ¼ cup of warm water until smooth. Season.

Score the baby squid with a sharp knife and combine in a bowl with lemon juice, garlic, olive oil and *dukkah*, cover and leave to marinate in the fridge for 20 minutes.

Grill (broil) the squid on a barbecue (grill) for 1–2 minutes on each side.

Spoon some of the baba ghanouj onto each plate and place the hot cooked squid on top, accompany with the chopped herbs and drizzle with the dukkah dressing. Serve immediately.

SERVES 3

Everyone cooks potatoes differently—I prefer to cook them in their skins because I find it's the only way to retain the full flavour and stop them from getting dry when baked, floury when boiled and watery when steamed. Once cool enough to touch, peel off the skin or scoop out the flesh.

MAAKOUDA
POTATO CROQUETTES

6 Pontiac or Desiree potatoes, boiled
Salt and pepper, to taste
½ cup (125ml/4fl oz) milk
1 tablespoon crushed cumin seeds
3 cloves garlic, crushed
1 tablespoon chopped parsley
2 tablespoons chopped coriander (cilantro)
1½ cups plain flour
Pinch saffron thread
3 eggs
½ cup warm water
Olive oil

Place the cooked potato in a large bowl and allow to cool for 10 minutes. Season then mash until there are no large lumps.

Heat the milk in a large frypan without boiling, add the mashed potato and stir with a wooden spoon whilst adding the cumin, garlic, parsley and coriander.

Remove from the heat and refrigerate the mix for 30 minutes or until cold. Mould the cold mix into 5cm (2ins) logs that are approximately 3cm thick and 2cm wide (1in x ¾in) or into flat patty shapes. Set aside.

Whisk together the flour, saffron, eggs and warm water and leave to stand for an hour.

Heat enough olive oil for deep-frying in a large frying pan on a high heat. Dip the potato croquettes into the batter and place into the hot oil, cooking until golden brown on both sides.

Remove with a slotted spoon and drain on paper towels.

Serve warm with lemon wedges, *harissa* and yoghurt or some olives.

SERVES 2

PRESERVED LEMONS & LIMES

PRESERVED LEMONS AND LIMES FORM THE BASIS
FOR MANY RECIPES IN MOROCCAN COOKING.

MOROCCAN PRESERVED LIMES
MOROCCAN PRESERVED LIMES

MOROCCAN PRESERVED LIMES

15 fresh limes
1½ cups sea salt (not ground)
6 kaffir lime leaves
1 tablespoon green peppercorns
4 cardamom pods
3 limes, juiced

Wash and scrub the limes then dry.

Over a large bowl to catch the juices, cut 3 deep pockets into the sides of the limes, being careful not to cut right through them. Fill the pockets generously with the sea salt.

Pack the limes as best you can into a 2 litre (3½ pint) jar, or two 1 litre (1¾ pints) jars.

To the bowl of collected lime juice and fallen salt, add the kaffir leaves, peppercorns, cardamom pods and lime juice. Pour over the limes and close the lid tightly. If the limes don't all fit in at first, press down on them firmly and leave for a couple of hours. Eventually the juices will fill up the jar, add more limes until the juice then reaches the top of the jar.

Leave the jar to stand at room temperature overnight.

MAKES 2 LITRES (3½ PINTS)

NOTE
The next day there may be room for more limes. Always make sure the limes are covered in liquid. Once the jar is full ensure it is tightly sealed and refrigerate for at least 3 weeks before use to prevent mould from occurring.

Preserved limes can last at least a year and a half if not longer, as long as they're correctly preserved.

This is a typical Marrakech dish, named, like the tajine, after the vessel it is cooked in—a large earthenware vase-shaped pot with a round base, an open neck and a handle on each side. There is no particular way of preparing this tasty dish other than to throw in all the ingredients and cook and for this reason tangia is traditionally made by men for men (it is known as the bachelor dish) but is also favoured by students and busy people. In Morocco the filled tangia is brought to the hammam (Turkish baths) and taken into a special room where the farnachi (the man who tends the fire) covers it in hot ashes and leaves it to cook for about 8 hours. It is also taken to the communal oven and left overnight, though in reality in only needs to cook for 2–3 hours.

TANGIA MARAKECHIA

TANGIA MARAKECHIA
TANGIA MARAKECHIA

1.5kg (3lbs) oxtail, cut in 7cm (2¾in) pieces
100g (3½oz) smen, aged butter (or blue cheese)
2 Spanish onions, peeled and coarsely grated
3 cloves garlic, finely peeled and chopped
½ bunch parsley, finely chopped
½ bunch coriander, finely chopped
1 preserved lemon, quartered
1 teaspoon ras el hanout
3 large tomatoes, seeded (pitted) and diced
1 pinch of saffron thread
½ teaspoon powdered ginger
1 teaspoon sweet paprika
500ml (16fl oz) water
Salt and pepper, to taste

Place all ingredients into the clean tangia, cover with baking paper or aluminium foil and tie with string around the neck, shake to mix then poke holes through the top.

Leave to cook over hot coal and ashes for about 5–6 hours.

If you can't get a tangia, place all ingredients into a flameproof casserole, stir well and cover with a tight fitting lid. Cook in a pre-heated slow oven, 150°C (300°F) Gas Mark 2 for 2–3 hours or on the stove over a low heat for at least 3 hours.

Serve hot with couscous or bread.

SERVES 6

MOROCCAN BAKED FISH

MOROCCAN BAKED FISH

MOROCCAN BAKED FISH

2 cloves garlic, crushed
2.5cm (1in) piece ginger root, grated
1 teaspoon cumin
1 teaspoon hot paprika
½ teaspoon coriander (cilantro) seeds
1 cup flat leaf parsley
1 cup fresh coriander
¼ cup (60ml/2fl oz) olive oil
Saffron threads, pinch
Zest of 1 lemon
Ground cinnamon, pinch
½ cup (125ml/4fl oz) orange juice
1kg (2lbs) fish, (either Blue Eye, Whiting or Snapper), cut in to 4 steaks
Salt, pinch
½ preserved lemon, sliced for garnish and marinade

Preheat oven to hot, 220°C (450°F) Gas Mark 6.

Combine garlic, ginger, cumin, hot paprika, coriander seeds and the parsley and coriander leaves in a mortar and pestle. Grind and stir until you have made a paste.

Heat the olive oil in a saucepan, fry the paste and after 1 minute add the saffron, lemon zest, cinnamon and orange juice to make a smooth sauce.

Rub the fish with the salt and half the preserved lemon slices and place in a greased shallow baking dish. Cook in the oven for 10 minutes or until cooked through.

Place the fish on a warm plate and spoon over the smooth sauce, garnish with the remaining preserved lemon and serve straight away.

SERVES 4

MOROCCAN PRESERVED LEMONS

MOROCCAN PRESERVED LEMONS

MOROCCAN PRESERVED LEMONS

10 thin skinned lemons
1½ cups (480g/16½oz) rock salt
1 litre (32fl oz) boiling water
1 lemon, juiced
8 cardamom pods
2 small red chillies, optional
2 bay leaves, optional
Olive oil, to cover

Scrub the lemons well and soak in water for about 3 days, changing the water daily (this disperses the gas and acids contained in the fruit). Remove from the water and cut four pockets end to end into each lemon, being careful not to slice right through.

Holding a lemon over a bowl (to catch any juice and salt), fill the pockets generously with rock salt, and arrange in a 2 litres (64fl oz) preserving jar. Repeat with remaining lemons.

Cover the lemons with boiling water. Add the leftover salt and juice, lemon juice and cardamom pods. Chillies and bay leaves may also be added for flavour and decoration, if you like.

Leave the jar for a few minutes to ensure that most of the air bubbles are released. Pour over a thin layer of olive oil to cover the surface. Seal tightly, and store for at least 1 month prior to use.

Correctly preserved lemons can be stored for years.

MAKES 10

NOTE
Alternatively, you could put these into 2 x 1 litre (32fl oz) jars.

CHARMOULA MARINADE

CHARMOULA MARINADE
CHARMOULA MARINADE

1 tablespoon dried crushed chilli
1 tablespoon sweet paprika
1 teaspoon chopped fresh ginger
½ teaspoon saffron threads
2 onions, diced
2 bay leaves
1 tablespoon ground cumin
2 garlic cloves, chopped
2 tablespoons chopped flat leaf parsley
2 tablespoons chopped coriander (cilantro)
½ preserved lemon, sliced thinly
½ cup (125ml/4fl oz) olive oil
½ lemon, juiced

Mix all the ingredients together thoroughly, and leave for half an hour prior to use. The charmoula can be stored in the refrigerator for up to 7 days.

MAKES ABOUT 3 CUPS

SAFFRON

PRECIOUS GOLD

Saffron is one of the few things that truly is worth its weight in gold—a delicate spice with a beautiful golden colour made from the tiny red stigma, once called eagle's blood by King Solomon, in the centre of the purple crocus flower. It has been cultivated for thousands of years for use in medicines, perfumes and dyes and as a wonderful flavouring in dishes.

Although the origins of saffron are confusing, it is thought that it comes from the Orient because its cultivation was widely spread in Asia Minor many thousands of years ago. One of the first historic references to the use of saffron comes from ancient Egypt, where it was used by Cleopatra as an aromatic and seductive essence for her body and to cleanse temples and sacred places.

Saffron is called *azafran* in Spanish and is a spice that has a special place in history. At one point it was even used as currency. In ancient Greece it was used as a remedy for sleeplessness and to reduce hangovers. It was also used to perfume bathing and as an aphrodisiac and women used it as a cosmetic because of its colouring and aromatic properties. The Roman Emperor Nero had the streets covered with it for his parades, Phoenicians made veils of it for their brides and Buddhists used it to dye their robes.

Arabs used saffron in medicine for its anaesthetic properties. It was the Arabs who introduced saffron to Morocco in the 9th century and started its cultivation in Spain in the 10th century. Evidence shows that it was an irreplaceable ingredient in the Hispanic Arabic cooking of the time.

It was introduced to the West through doctors such as Razi and Ibn Sina. During the Middle Ages, saffron became well known in Great Britain. The legend says that in the period of Edward III, a pilgrim brought a bulb of saffron hidden in a hole in his stick from the Middle East to the town of Walden. There the bulb was grown and reproduced giving prosperity to the town to this day known as Saffron Walden.

During the renaissance, Venice stood out as the most important commercial centre for saffron. At that time it was literally worth its weight in gold and even today it is still the most expensive spice in the world.

Saffron continues to be used widely for flavouring food and as a dye for cloth in underdeveloped countries and among back-to-basics artisans. Traditional uses of saffron include use as a sedative, expectorant, aphrodisiac, and diaphoretic (to induce perspiration). Anecdotal reports from the tropical regions of Asia describe the use of a paste composed of sandalwood and saffron as a soothing balm for dry skin. Between the 16th and 19th centuries, saffron was used for pain relief in various preparations such as laudanum which contained sherry wine, opium, saffron, cinnamon, and cloves and 'black-drop' with opium, nutmeg, saffron, and yeast.

My experience of saffron is of its enigmatic characteristics; the lightest perfume, the lightest taste that can be destroyed by greed and the fragile texture. Its effect on food reminds me of the warmth of the Moroccan sun.

I went to visit the saffron fields and watch the processing in Morocco's saffron capital, Talouine in Southern Morocco. I was shown around by one of the farmers, a manager working for Dr Abdelaziz Laqbaqbi, a prominent figure in the saffron industry. As I walked through the fields of stunning exuberant purple, I was told that one hectare of these flowers would make just one kilo of saffron thread. Of course I've always known what saffron really is but seeing first hand the amount of work that goes into production made the immense value of saffron became even more vivid. It is estimated that it takes some 14,000 stigmas to produce only one ounce of saffron threads. The labour-intensive process makes the cost of these bright red threads very high but luckily a little bit goes a long way and you can buy enough for a number of meals for very little.

Saffron is readily available in most large grocery stores and specialty markets. Due to its value, it may be stocked in a locked or secured area, so if you don't see any on the shelf, ask the manager. Choose saffron threads or powder from a reputable distributor. Saffron should be packaged in foil to protect from air and light. Bulk saffron is often sold from small wooden boxes. Your best bet is to go with the threads which are the whole stigmas. Not only will they retain their flavour longer, but you will also be assured you have purchased pure saffron. Powdered saffron is not as strong, tends to lose flavour, and is also easily adulterated with fillers and imitations, such as turmeric. Since so little is needed, you will find ground saffron sold in packets of about 1/16 of a teaspoon and threads equalling about ½ a teaspoon.

Store saffron in an airtight container in a cool, dark place for up to six months. Like other herbs and spices it is sensitive to light, so wrap the packet in foil to protect it. It will not spoil but it will lose more and more of its flavour with age.

SAFFRON PREPARATION

One teaspoon of saffron strands will yield 250ml (8fl oz) of prepared saffron and, once prepared as below, can be kept in the refrigerator for three or four weeks.

Heat a dry frypan on low heat and toast the threads very slowly, stirring continuously with a wooden spoon for 2 minutes. When the saffron strands have reached a deep red colour, put them straight away in to a wooden mortar or bowl and while they are still hot crush them very finely. Pour the powder into a dry jar, and fill the jar with 250ml (8 fl oz) of warm water. Close it tightly and shake thoroughly to allow all the saffron powder to dilute in the water. The water immediately takes on a beautiful orange colour. Leave to cool and refrigerate. Always shake the jar before use.

SAFFRON COUSCOUS WITH

SAFFRON COUSCOUS WITH
LAMB SHANK AND TFAIA

LAMB SHANK AND TFAIA

Sauce
2 tablespoons olive oil
500g (1lb) lamb shank
2 onions, chopped
½ tablespoon salt
¼ tablespoon ginger
1 tablespoon cumin
1 tablespoon orange blossom water
150g (5oz) chickpeas
1 bunch parsley
1 litre (1¾ pints) water
¼ tablespoon saffron
1 tablespoon *smen* (aged butter)

Couscous
50ml (2fl oz) water
½ tablespoon salt
¼ tablespoon saffron
500g (1lb) couscous
1 tablespoon *smen* (aged butter) or
   blue cheese

Tfaia
2 onions, sliced julienne
100g (3½oz) butter
100g (3½oz) raisins
½ tablespoon salt
50g (2oz) sugar
1 tablespoon cinnamon powder
1 tablespoon orange blossom water

In the bottom of a *couscousier* or a pan with a steamer heat the oil and lightly fry the lamb and onions.

Add the salt, ginger, cumin, orange blossom water, chickpeas and parsley. Cover with water and gently bring to boil.

Take out 3–4 ladles of the sauce and combine with *smen* and saffron in a casserole dish. Set aside to use in the *tfaia*.

Place the next level of the steamer over the simmering lamb. In a separate saucepan combine the water, salt and saffron and heat to almost boiling point.

Place the couscous in a shallow bowl and cover with the saffron water. Allow to soak up the liquid for 5–10 minutes.

Using a wooden spoon gently stir the couscous, then use your fingers to separate the grains and rub out all the lumps.

Spread evenly in to the second level of the steamer and steam for 10 minutes until steam begins to come through the couscous.

Remove couscous from the steamer and place into a large bowl working the grains well with your fingers to separate. Add *smen* and more of the saffron water. Return to steamer and cook again until steam begins to rise through the couscous.

Meanwhile make the *tfaia* by frying the onions in butter and salt. Add in the reserved *smen* and saffron sauce, cook and reduce for 15 minutes. Add raisins, sugar, cinnamon and orange blossom water. Reduce until colour becomes brown.

To serve, place the couscous around the outside of a heated serving plate. Place lamb shanks in the centre and top with a little of the sauce. Top with the sweet saffron *tfaia* and sesame seeds. Extra sauce can be served from the meat pot and extra *tfaia* can be served as a side dish.

SERVES 4

SAFFRON *BADINJAL*

SAFFRON *BADINJAL*
SAFFRON EGGPLANT

SAFFRON EGGPLANT

2½ medium eggplants (aubergines)
1 tablespoon olive oil
1 tablespoon prepared saffron
1 tablespoon fresh mint leaves
1 tablespoon lemon juice
1 tablespoon cumin
Salt and pepper, to taste

Saffron Dressing
2 tablespoons tahini
2 cloves garlic, sliced
1 tablespoon prepared saffron liquid
1 tablespoon fresh mint leaves
1 tablespoon fresh thyme leaves
Salt and pepper, to taste
½ cup (125ml/4fl oz) vegetable stock
2 tablespoons olive oil
2 tablespoons lemon juice

Salad
1 small red capsicum (bell pepper)
1 small green capsicum
2 medium tomatoes, poached, peeled and pitted
1 tablespoon coriander (cilantro) leaves
1 teaspoon cumin seeds
2 tablespoons olive oil
1 tablespoon white vinegar
Salt and pepper, to taste

Preheat the oven to moderate, 180°C (350°F) Gas Mark 4.

Halve the eggplants and brush with oil, place the 5 halves on a metal tray lined with baking paper and bake for 20 minutes or until soft to touch.

When cool enough to handle, peel off the skin leaving the stalks on. Blend the saffron, mint, lemon juice, cumin and seasoning in a food processor to make a saffron mint paste. Brush this over 4 of the eggplant halves. Set aside.

Blend the 5th eggplant half, tahini, garlic, prepared saffron, mint, thyme, salt and pepper in a food processor. While it's mixing, slowly poor in the vegetable stock. When blended, add in the olive oil and lemon juice a teaspoon each at a time until you've used all of it, as if you were making mayonnaise. Set aside.

Roast the capsicums on a hot chargrill or over a flame for a few minutes until blistered and blackened on all sides. Place in a plastic bag for a few minutes to sweat, then peel off the skin, halve, remove seeds and membrane and dice the flesh into small pieces.

Dice the tomato flesh to the same size as the capsicum.

Mix together the capsicum, tomato and coriander.

Toast the cumin seeds, roughly crush in a mortar and pestle and mix in with the vegetables while the aroma is still fresh.

Pour in the olive oil and vinegar and season with salt and pepper.

Place each eggplant half on a large flat dish. Slice 4 times lengthways stopping before the top to form a fan shape.

Drizzle over zigzags of the saffron dressing and serve with the salad.

SERVES 4 AS AN ENTREE

SAFFRON AND NUT RICE

SAFFRON AND NUT RICE
SAFFRON AND NUT RICE

350g (11oz) long grain rice (preferably jasmine rice)
50g (2oz) butter
50g (2oz) blue cheese
80g (2½oz) walnuts, chopped
80g (2½oz) pine nuts
80g (2½oz) almonds, chopped
80g (2½oz) cashews, chopped
2 tablespoons prepared saffron liquid
½ tablespoon ground ginger
100g (3½oz) seedless raisins
Salt, to taste
½ litre (500ml/16fl oz) hot water

Wash the rice under cold running water and drain well.

Melt the butter in a flameproof casserole dish on the stove over a low heat, crumble in the cheese and add the rice, stir until the grains are well coated.

Stir in all the nuts, salt, saffron and ground ginger and cook over low heat until the rice becomes translucent.

Mix in the raisins, season and pour in the hot water, cover and simmer for 20 minutes until the water has been absorbed.

Once cooked, fluff the rice and garnish with mint leaves if you desire.

SERVES 4

The best way to buy mussels is fresh and alive, although they are also sold cooked and preserved in either oil or sauce. When you're buying fresh they must be tightly closed or snap shut when tapped; this shows they're still alive and edible. You should cook them within three days of being caught.

SAFFRON MUSSELS CASSOLETTES

SAFFRON MUSSELS CASSOLETTES

SAFFRON MUSSELS CASSOLETTES

1kg (2lbs) mussels (clams), in their shells
1 shallot (spring onion), chopped
1 bulb fennel, very finely chopped
100ml (3fl oz) white wine
20g (¾oz) blue cheese
20g (¾oz) butter
2 tablespoons plain flour
3 eggs
2 tablespoons prepared saffron
½ bunch parsley, chopped

Preheat the oven to slow, 140°C (280°F) Gas Mark 2.

It's important to make sure the mussels are completely cleaned before use. Remove everything attached to them and brush and scrape the shells under cold water.

In a casserole dish over a hot stove, cook the shallots and fennel with the wine and blue cheese until melted and combined.

Add in the mussels, stir and then cook over a low heat with a lid on for 5 minutes, until they are half cooked.

Brush two *cassolette* dishes with the butter and coat with the flour.

Remove the mussels from the sauce with a slotted spoon and place them in the base of the dishes.

Take the sauce off the heat.

Separate the eggs and gently mix the yolks into the hot sauce then add the saffron.

In a separate bowl, beat the egg whites until they form stiff peaks, delicately stir the egg whites into the hot sauce while maintaining a fluffy texture.

Gently cover the mussels with the saffron mousse.

Bake for 10 minutes.

This must be served immediately like a soufflé, and garnish with chopped parsley.

SERVES 2

SAFFRON TEA

SAFFRON TEA
SAFFRON TEA

5 g (¹/₆oz) Chinese green tea
1 litre (1¾ pints) water, boiling
Pinch saffron threads
40g (1½oz) sugar or honey

Place the tea leaves in teapot with a ¼ cup of the boiling water, let soak for 30 seconds, then pour out the water leaving the leaves in the pot. This gets rid of the initial bitterness of the leaves. Pour enough boiling water to fill the pot and leave to infuse for 3–5 minutes, and then add the saffron and sugar.

Pour out a glass, then pour back into the pot. Repeat this a few times.

Leave to infuse for 20 minutes. Serve hot.

SERVES 1

Enjoy these delicious biscuits with mint tea.

PALETS AU SAFFRON

¼ tablespoon saffron powder
2 tablespoons milk
1 egg yolk
80g (2½oz) butter
40g (1½oz) caster sugar
50g (2oz) almond meal
150g (5oz) plain flour

Glaze
1 tablespoon butter
1 tablespoon orange blossom water
Small pinch affron powder

In a small bowl or cup, mix the saffron powder with the milk and allow to soak for 1 hour.

Preheat the oven to moderate, 160°C (325°F) Gas Mark 3.

In a large bowl, mix together the egg yolk, butter, sugar and saffron milk.

Add in the almond meal and plain flour, mixing until you get a dough-like consistency.

Scoop out teaspoon sized balls of mix onto lined oven trays.

Mix together the butter, orange blossom and saffron powder and brush this over the biscuits, then bake for 15 minutes or until golden brown.

Cool completely before eating.

MAKES 12 BISCUITS

SALADS

MIDDLE EASTERN SALAD

MIDDLE EASTERN SALAD

MIDDLE EASTERN SALAD

250g (8oz) haloumi cheese, cut into 1cm (½in) slices
1 teaspoon *zaatar*
250g (8oz) mixed lettuce leaves
½ cup pitted green olives
100g (3½oz) cooked chickpeas
½ cup (125ml/4fl oz) olive oil
8 small cooked felafel, halved
¹/₃ cup hummus
1 tablespoon crushed toasted cumin
½ preserved lemon
¼ cup toasted pine nuts
Salt and pepper, to taste

Rub the haloumi with *zaatar*. Set aside.

Wash and drain the mixed leaves theN toss with the olives and chickpeas and place in a large serving bowl.

Heat 2 tablespoons of the olive oil in a pan and fry the felafel halves until toasted, then throw into the salad.

In the same pan add another tablespoon of the olive oil and pan fry the haloumi until golden brown on both sides, then add to the salad.

In a food processor or blender, combine the hummus, remaining olive oil, cumin and preserved lemon until well blended. Drizzle over the salad.

Sprinkle over the pine nuts, season and serve.

SERVES 4 AS A SIDE DISH OR ENTREE

GOATS CHEESE, DATE
AND FIG SALAD

GOATS CHEESE, DATE
AND FIG SALAD

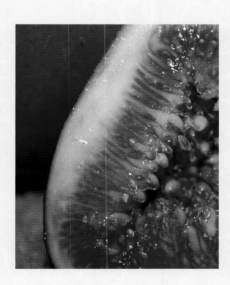

Salad
100g (3½oz) mixed baby salad leaves
100g (3½oz) witlof leaves
1 cup fresh dates, halved and pitted
3 green apples, cored and thinly sliced
4 fresh figs, quartered
½ cup chopped walnuts
200g (6½oz) soft goat cheese

Dressing
2 tablespoons raisins
½ cup (60ml/2fl oz) honey
½ cup (60ml/2fl oz) apple cider
1 strip lemon rind
2 tablespoons lemon juice
½ cup (60ml/2fl oz) extra virgin olive oil

Mix the baby leaves, witlof, dates and apple slices together and put into a large shallow bowl.

Arrange the fig pieces around the edges and sprinkle the walnuts on top of the salad.

Roughly crumble the goat's cheese over, mainly in the middle.

For the dressing, place all ingredients except the lemon juice and oil in a food processor or blender. While blending, pour in the lemon juice and olive oil, teaspoon by teaspoon, blend until smooth and combined.

Drizzle dressing over the salad and serve. Sprinkle with grinded rock salt to taste if necessary.

SERVES 4

CHEKCHOUKA

CHEKCHOUKA
ROASTED BELL PEPPER
AND TOMATO SALAD

AND TOMATO SALAD

2 green capsicums (bell peppers)
2 red capsicum
4 tomatoes
1/3 cup (80ml/2½fl oz) olive oil
1 garlic clove, crushed
1 teaspoon ground cumin
½ bunch coriander (cilantro), finely chopped
½ bunch flat parsley, finely chopped
Salt and pepper, to taste

Roast the capsicums on a hot chargrill or over a flame for a few minutes until blistered and blackened on all sides. Place in a plastic bag for a few minutes to sweat, then peel off the skin, halve, remove seeds and membrane and dice the flesh into small pieces.

Plunge tomatoes in boiling water for 1–2 minutes and drain (this way the tomatoes remain raw and fresh with flavour). Cut into 6 segments and lay skin-side down on a board. To remove skin use a sharp knife directed away from you to cut between the flesh and the skin so that the skin is removed in one piece. Slice off the seeds and dice or cut into julienne and add to the capsicum.

Heat the olive oil in a heavy pan, add the garlic, cumin, capsicum and tomatoes, coriander and parsley. Simmer for 5 minutes on low heat and adjust the seasoning of salt and pepper to taste.

Serve cold.

SERVES 4 AS A SIDE DISH OR ENTREE

SWEET CUCUMBER SALAD

SWEET CUCUMBER SALAD
SWEET CUCUMBER SALAD

500g (1lb) cucumber (whichever type you prefer), washed
100g (3½oz) caster sugar
1 tablespoon orange blossom water
1 lemon, juiced
1 orange, juiced
1 teaspoon fresh thyme

Shred the cucumber on the small blades of a grater.

Place in a large salad bowl and combine with the sugar, orange blossom water and citrus juices.

Mix well and serve cold, garnished with thyme.

SERVES 4 AS A SIDE DISH

CARAMELISED TOMATOES

CARAMELISED TOMATOES
CARAMELISED TOMATOES

10 ripe tomatoes
70g (2oz) butter
1 teaspoon salt
1 tablespoon caster sugar
Pinch grated nutmeg
2 tablespoons rosewater
½ teaspoon ground pepper
2 tablespoons honey
½ teaspoon ground cinnamon
Roasted sesame seeds or crushed almonds for garnish

Place tomatoes in enough boiling water to cover for 2 minutes. Drain. Cut a cross at the stem end and peel off the skin. De-seed and dice.

Melt butter in heavy frypan, add tomatoes, salt, sugar, nutmeg and rosewater. Mix over high heat then simmer for 30 minutes or until all the liquid is absorbed. Add pepper, honey and cinnamon. Mix well and continue cooking for 10 minutes.

Serve hot or cold, garnished with roasted sesame seeds or crushed almonds.

SERVES 4 AS A SIDE DISH

BASTOURMA AND
POMEGRANATE SALAD

Dressing
2 tablespoons pomegranate molasses
1 tablespoon icing sugar
1 ruby grapefruit, juiced
1 tablespoon argan oil
Salt and cracked pepper, to taste

4 heads baby fennel, trimmed, sliced thinly and soaked in ice water
250g (8oz) bastourma, thinly sliced
1 bunch fresh mint, torn
150g (5oz) Parmesan cheese, shaved
1 cup pomegranate seeds

Combine the pomegranate molasses, sugar, grapefruit juice, oil, salt and pepper in a screw top jar and shake vigorously.
Drain the fennel and place in a salad bowl with the bastourma, mint leaves and Parmesan cheese.
Toss gently to combine.
Top with the pomegranate seeds and place on a large serving plate or divide into individual bowls.
Drizzle with dressing and serve immediately.

SERVES 2

OOA (OUT OF AFRICA) SALSA

OOA (OUT OF AFRICA) SALSA

OOA (OUT OF AFRICA) SALSA

2 red capsicums (bell peppers)
4 Roma tomatoes
200g (6½oz)piece butternut pumpkin (butternut squash)
1 tablespoon honey
2 ruby grapefruit
10 basil leaves
10 mint leaves
½ bunch coriander (cilantro)
4 tablespoons olive oil
1 tablespoon red wine vinegar
Salt and freshly ground black pepper, to taste

Preheat the oven to moderate 180°C (350°F) Gas Mark 4. Cut the capsicums into large flat pieces, discarding the seeds and membrane. Grill (broil) skin side up, until the skin is black. Peel and cut into 1cm (³/₈in) squares.

Make a small slit in the skin of the tomatoes, and plunge into boiling water. Dip into cold water then peel away the skin. Cut in half lengthways, seed and cut into 1cm (³/₈in) dices.

Cut the pumpkin into 1cm (³/₈in) cubes. Coat in honey and put into a shallow roasting dish. Roast for 10–15 minutes until golden, take out and cool.

Peel the grapefruit, making sure to remove all the white pith. Cut into 1cm (³/₈in) cubes.

Combine the capsicum, tomatoes, pumpkin and grapefruit in a glass bowl and gently mix together. Chop the herbs and add just before serving. Whisk the oil and vinegar with salt and pepper, and drizzle over the salsa.

SERVES 4

ARTICHOKES

WILD HEART

The artichoke is a big thistle plant and a member of the sunflower family, which grows wild in the south of Europe and is cultivated in the United States, primarily in California. The long, spiny leaves grow from the base of the up to 1 metre (3 foot) high stems up to the large heads of violet or white thistle-like flowers. The fleshy base from which these flowers rise and the leaves of the immature flower are the portions eaten.

According to an Aegean legend in song, the first artichoke was a lovely young girl who lived on the island of Zinari. The god, Zeus was visiting his brother Poseidon one day when, as he emerged from the sea, he spied a beautiful young mortal woman. She did not seem frightened by the presence of a god and Zeus seized the opportunity to seduce her. He was so pleased with the girl, who's name was Cynara, that he decided to make her a goddess so that she could be nearer to his home on Olympia. Cynara agreed to the promotion and Zeus anticipated the trysts whenever his wife Hera was away. However, Cynara soon missed her mother and grew homesick. She snuck back to the world of mortals for a brief visit. Zeus found out after she returned and enraged, he hurled her back to earth and transformed her into the plant we know as the artichoke.

Ancient Greeks and Romans considered artichokes a delicacy and an aphrodisiac. In ancient Greece, eating artichoke was thought to secure the birth of a boy. In 77AD, the Roman naturalist Caius Plinius Secundus or Pliny the Elder, called the choke 'one of the earth's monstrosities'. Evidently though he and his colleagues continued to enjoy eating them preserved in honey, vinegar and cumin, so that the treat would be available year round.

From about 800AD, North African Moors begin cultivating artichokes in the area of Granada, Spain, and another Arab group, the Saracens, grew them in Sicily. This may explain why the English word artichoke is derived from the Arabic *al'qarshuf*, rather than from the Latin, *cynara*. Between 800 and 1500AD, it's probable that the artichoke was improved, perhaps in monastery gardens, into the plant we would recognise today.

Always choose artichoke globes that are dark green, heavy, and have 'tight' leaves, not dry looking or turning brown. If the leaves appear too open then the choke is past its prime. You can still eat them, but the leaves may be tough, although they're still fine for artichoke soup. Baby artichokes are fully mature artichokes that grow closer to the ground, sheltered by the larger leaves on the plant. They are easy to cook and prepare because the inner fuzzy portion of the choke does not develop. Fresh artichokes should be put unwashed in to a plastic bag, refrigerated and used within 4 days of purchase. If you grow your own then cook them straight after picking.

Artichoke eating is a hands-on affair and another case in life where 'the journey is as important as the destination'. Pull each leaf off the choke and hold the pointed end between your fingers and drag the leaf between your teeth. Most of the edible portion is on inside bottom third of the choke leaf. When you serve artichokes it's nice to put a bowl on the table for the discarded leaves.

Once you've eaten all the leaves you'll see the heart or flower of the choke. By the way, the leaves closest to the heart of the choke are very tender and depending on the size and age of the choke you can frequently eat the whole cluster of leaves. Once you see a bed of fuzzy or hair-like strands you've hit the heart. Scoop out the fuzz with a spoon and discard the rest. The base of the choke is edible and the favourite part of the artichoke for some people.

VEAL KNUCKLE TAJINE
WITH ARTICHOKES

1½kg (3lbs) artichokes
1 tablespoon vinegar
1kg (2lbs) green peas
1kg (2lbs) veal knuckle
1 teaspoon salt
1 teaspoon pepper
¼ cup (60ml/2fl oz) olive oil
1 brown onion
1 tablespoon crushed garlic
1 ripe tomato, diced
1 teaspoon ground ginger
½ teaspoon saffron colour
1 saffron thread
2 bay leaves
1 cinnamon stick
½ cup green olives
1 preserved lemon, cut into 8 wedges

Prepare artichokes, keeping only the hearts which you then soak in a bowl of water and vinegar. Either shell peas or soak frozen peas in warm water.

Cut meat into 150g (5oz) pieces, season with salt and pepper. Heat oil in large fry pan and sauté meat first, then add onion, garlic, tomato, ginger, saffron, bay leaves and cinnamon stick, stirring all the time. Cover with 1 litre (32fl oz) water and simmer for 1/2 hour, stirring from time to time.

Once meat is tender and breaks apart easily, add peas and simmer for 10 minutes, adding more water if necessary. Add artichoke hearts and simmer for 5 minutes. Turn off heat and transfer to a large tajine.

Place veal in middle, surround with veggies, add green olives and preserved lemon on top and cook on low heat for 10 minutes with tajine lid on.

Serve while steaming hot.

SERVES 4

TO CLEAN AND PREPARE AN ARTICHOKE FOR COOKING

- Tap the artichoke upside down in the sink to remove any insects. With most commercially grown chokes this is not usually an issue, but if you or a friend grow artichokes organically you'll find earwigs love to live in the leaves.
- Rinse the choke under running water.
- I prefer not to cut away the entire stem because it tastes good—I leave about 3½cm (1½ins). You may remove the entire stem at the base, if you prefer. Trim the end and peel the top layer off the stem. Remove the really small leaves along the bottom of the choke. Some people whack off the top inch or so to remove the thistles and to even out the top before stuffing. You may also use scissors or a sharp knife to trim away the sharp tips. Before cooking, prepared artichokes should be placed in a bowl of water with the juice of one or two lemons.

METHOD A WITH STEM

1 Cut off the stalk about 4cm (1½inches) from the leaves and remove the large outer leaves.
2 Remove large leaves.
3 Cut away the small clump leaving only the bottom (can be replaced when the choke has been discarded).
4 Use a small teaspoon to scoop out the hairy part of the choke. Place in a bowl of water with lemon juice.

METHOD B WITHOUT STEM

1 Discard the coarse outer leaves from each artichoke.
2 Cut off the stalk, at the end closest to the leaves and rub with the lemon every time you make a cut.
3 Cut the clump of leaves in half sideways. Pull out the hair leaving a cup.
4 Squeeze lemon juice over the heart and place in a bowl of water with lemon juice.

METHOD A

METHOD B

ARTICHOKE HEART WITH CARAMELISED SCALLOPS, SALMON AND BEETROOT RELISH

Beetroot Relish
1 large beetroot, finely grated
1 tablespoon lemon juice
2 teaspoons ginger, finely chopped

4 globe artichoke hearts
160g (5oz) fresh salmon
1tsp rock salt
1tbsp extra virgin olive oil
1 tablespoon salted butter
1 tablespoon crushed garlic
1 tablespoon brown sugar
Salt and pepper, to taste
4 large fresh scallops
100g (3oz) goat cheese

Dressing
1 cup (150g/5oz) semi-dried tomatoes
2 preserved lemons, flesh only
1 cup 45g/1½oz basil leaves
1 tablespoon freshly ground pepper
1 tablespoon sea salt
½ teaspoon saffron threads
1 tablespoon sugar
2 cups (500ml/16fl oz) extra virgin olive oil
1 cup red wine vinegar

Combine the relish ingredients together in a bowl and set aside.

To make the dressing, combine the tomatoes, lemon flesh, basil, pepper, salt, saffron and sugar in a food processor until smooth. With the motor running, gradually add the olive oil and vinegar, a little at a time. Continue to process until smooth again.

Soak the artichoke hearts in a bowl of cold water with the lemon juice until you are ready to cook them.

Steam the salmon over simmering water until cooked through although still darker pink in the middle. Cut the fish into 4 pieces.

Boil the artichoke hearts with the salt and olive oil for about ten minutes, they should still be slightly firm to the touch.

Over a low heat melt the butter in a frypan and sizzle the garlic, add in the sugar and stir until all is melted and combined. Add the salt and pepper and flash fry the scallops on each side, coating them with the sauce.

Place an artichoke heart cut side up in the centre of each serving plate, place one scallop on top of each and spoon over a tablespoon of goats cheese. Add the salmon to the plate, garnish with a spoonful of the beetroot relish.

Drizzle over with sundried tomato and preserved lemon dressing.

SERVES 4 AS A STARTER

POMEGRANATES

ANCIENT FRUIT

This ancient fruit has garnered a lot of attention recently. And for good reason—pomegranates are sensuous, healthy and have a gorgeous colour. They also have a five thousand year history, delicious juicy seeds and documented health benefits. Little wonder that this fruit of old is back—they're also my favourite!

The pomegranate was carried by Arabian caravans along with other trade goods, spices and water. The pomegranate's leathery skin allowed long storage and made the fruit an important and easy to carry fluid replacement as it contains up to 80 percent water and also the minerals sodium, potassium, calcium, iron and phosphorus that travellers lost in sweat as they crossed the hot deserts. Pomegranates were also generally grown in the settlements they visited.

The pomegranate was highly symbolic in ancient times. The Greek legend of Persephone is one of the most evocative stories about the pomegranate. Persephone was abducted and secretly given six pomegranate seeds while she was in the underworld. Because she had tasted the fruit in Hades, she was banished to the realm of darkness in winter for a third of the year and only allowed to come forth into the light in spring where she remained until winter came around again.

In the Muslim Qu'uran the pomegranate is called the 'Fruit of Paradise' and mentioned often, for example in Ar-Rahman - 68-69, 'In them will be Fruits, and dates, and pomegranates: Then which of the favours of your Lord will you deny?' The Prophet Mohammed is said to have encouraged his followers to eat the fruit to purge envy and hatred. In Islam, the gardens of paradise hold pomegranates and it was traditionally believed to be important to eat every seed of a pomegranate as one couldn't be sure which one came from paradise.

In Arabic folklore and poetry it is the symbol of the fluid of life (the mother's breast) and in Jewish custom tradition has it that a pomegranate has 613 seeds to represent the 613 commandments in the Torah. The pomegranate symbol is woven into high priest's robes and is also mentioned in the 'Song of Solomon'. It is the symbol of fertility, relating to the first commandment of the Torah, 'to be fruitful and multiply'. The pomegranate is also mentioned in ancient Egyptian hieroglyphics as 'First among fruits'.

The pomegranate is native in areas from Iran to the Himalayas in northern India and was cultivated and naturalised over the whole Mediterranean region from ancient times. It is widely cultivated throughout India and the drier parts of Southeast Asia, Malaya, the East Indies and tropical Africa.

Pomegranate trees have attractive glossy green leaves, grow up to five metres high and like to be pruned; the current year's growth should be removed in late winter to promote dense growth. The plants produce orange, crinkly eight-petalled flowers from late spring to late summer. These are followed by the most extraordinary coloured and shaped fruit which appear like a shiny crown which starts small and grows to the size of a grapefruit.

The fruit can be eaten by deeply scoring several times vertically and then breaking it apart. The clusters of juice sacs are then lifted out and eaten. The sacs also make an attractive garnish when sprinkled on various dishes. Pomegranate fruits are most often consumed as juice and can be juiced in several ways. The sacs can be removed and put through a basket press or the juice can be extracted by using an ordinary orange juice squeezer. Another approach is to warm the fruit slightly and roll it between the hands to soften the interior. A hole is then cut in the stem end which is placed over a glass to let the juice run out with the occasional squeeze from time to time to help it along.

The juice can be used in a variety of ways; as a fresh juice, to make jellies, sorbets or sauces as well as to flavour cakes or baked apples. Pomegranate syrup is sold commercially as grenadine. The juice can also be made into a wine.

Due to its thick rind the fruit can be kept for up to six months. The rind also contains a high percentage of tannic acid and is sometimes used for tanning leather. Pomegranate rinds were once used to tan the famous Moroccan and Spanish leathers.

According to *Unani* (Graeco-Arabic) medicine, the ideal time to eat pomegranate is after lunch. Take out the seeds, sprinkle with a little salt and black pepper and swallow the juice after chewing the seeds. This way of eating is beneficial in chronic constipation and indigestion. It also soothes the nerves and stimulates the liver. Authorities of *Unani* also maintain that persons who do tedious mental work should eat the fruit in the late afternoon. Another way of using the fruit advantageously is to press out the juice, add a little sugar and drink it. This is thought to promote good health and refresh the brain.

Common names of the pomegranate are Granada (in Spanish) and Grenade (in French).

This sauce is beautiful hot over puddings, warm over ice-cream or chilled with fruit or in drinks, it's also a great topping on cakes once combined with gelatine.

POMEGRANATE COULI

½ litre (16fl oz) water
250g (8oz) pomegranate seeds
1 ruby grapefruit, skin removed and sliced
100g (3½oz) caster sugar
2 tablespoons pomegranate molasses (see note below)
¼ cup (60ml/2fl oz) grenadine
2 tablespoons orange blossom water

In a saucepan, simmer the water, pomegranate seeds, grapefruit and sugar over medium heat for 20 minutes.

Puree the sauce using a food processor or put through a fine sieve to strain, discarding the leftover pulp.

Return the sauce to the saucepan and add the molasses, grenadine and orange blossom water and simmer for another 10 minutes.

MAKES APPROXIMATELY 750ML (3 CUPS)

NOTE
Pomegranate molasses is available from Middle Eastern food stores.

This delicious sauce is perfect whether served hot with game meat or chilled with desserts.

PEACH, PLUM AND POMEGRANATE SAUCE

4 white peaches
4 blood plums
2 tablespoons palm sugar
¼ cup (60ml/2fl oz) apple cider
1 sweet cinnamon stick
4 cloves
1 teaspoon orange zest
1 teaspoon ground ginger
1 tablespoon pomegranate molasses (see note)

Plunge peaches into a saucepan of boiling water for about 1 minute. Remove and cool under running water. Peel, halve and remove the stones and slice into six segments.

Do the same with the plums. Set fruit aside

In a large saucepan, combine sugar, apple cider, cinnamon, cloves, orange zest and ginger and stir over a low heat until the sugar dissolves. Simmer for 5 minutes add peach and plum segments and stir. Add the pomegranate molasses and simmer for more than 10 minutes until tender.

Garnish with fresh pomegranate.

MAKES 1 LITRE (13/4 PINTS)

This recipe has strong natural colours, elegant ingredients and unusual flavours but is deceptively easy to make. Prepare it with love and impress your friends.

ROASTED PEAR WITH NUT CRUMBLE AND ROSE POMEGRANATE AND STRAWBERRY SAUCE

2 whole pears, peeled and halved
¼ cup macadamia nuts, roughly chopped
¼ cup almonds, roughly chopped
1 tablespoon rosewater
½ cup desiccated coconut
1 tablespoon raw organic honey

For the Sauce
1 pomegranate
Pinch saffron thread
2 punnets strawberries
1 tablespoon pure maple syrup
½ cup (125ml/4fl oz) hibiscus juice (or cranberry juice)
1 tablespoon rosewater
½ cup (125ml/4fl oz) water

Place the pears onto a lined baking tray.

In a bowl, combine the nuts, rosewater, coconut and honey to form a crumble, then scatter this over the pears, cover with foil and bake for 20 minutes.

In the meantime, place all the sauce ingredients except 1 punnet of the strawberries in a saucepan and cook for 15 minutes.

Cool, then blend until smooth.

Strain the sauce into a bowl.

Thickly slice the remaining strawberries and arrange on a serving plate, drizzle with the sauce and serve with the hot pear crumble.

SERVES 4

DESSERTS

DATE AND ORANGE BLOSSOM SHOTS

DATE AND ORANGE BLOSSOM SHOTS

150g (5oz) pitted dried dates
700ml (23fl oz) milk
20g (¾oz) almond meal
1 teaspoon cinnamon
1 tablespoon orange blossom water

Soak the dates overnight in 300ml (10fl oz) of the milk.

Transfer the dates and milk to a saucepan and bring to the boil, then allow to cool before pouring into a blender and blending until smooth.

Add in the almond meal, cinnamon, orange blossom water and remaining milk, blend until combined and pour into shot glasses and serve with Moroccan biscuits.

MAKES 900ML (30FL OZ) OR 30 SHOTS

When you buy fruit always feel for firmness and pick the juiciest and freshest looking pieces you can find. This salad can be served by itself or with another dessert and goes especially well with ice-cream.

CITRUS SALAD

CITRUS SALAD
CITRUS SALAD

1 grapefruit
1 lemon
2 oranges
2 limes
1 cup water
½ cup caster sugar
1 tablespoon orange blossom water
1 tablespoon prepared saffron
2 tablespoons fresh mint leaves

Zest the fruits, taking care to only remove the peel and not the white pith as this is bitter. Wash the zest.

Place the fruit in the fridge until needed.

In a saucepan, boil the water, sugar and zest. Lower the heat and simmer to reduce the liquid to the thickness of warm runny honey, being careful not to burn the sugar.

Add the orange blossom water and saffron, stir for one minute and take off the heat, leave to cool down.

Chill for two hours.

Peel the citrus fruits completely, removing all the pith and then carefully separate the fruit into segments.

Place the segments in to a glass bowl and combine with the chilled sauce.

Garnish with mint leaves.

MAKES 6 CUPS

GINGER ICE-CREAM

GINGER ICE-CREAM
GINGER ICE-CREAM

100g (3½oz) ginger, crushed
1 litre (1¾ pints) milk
5 egg yolks
140g (4½oz) caster sugar
30g (1oz) milk powder
150ml (5fl oz) cream

Infuse the ginger in the milk overnight.

The next day, mix egg yolks and sugar until blended.

Cook milk powder and cream with infused milk and egg and sugar mix until boiling then immediately remove from the heat.

Transfer to a metal bowl, boil a pan of water and place the bowl with the ice-cream mixture over it.

Beat the mix for 5 minutes then place in the freezer overnight, or into an ice-cream maker.

MAKES 11/2 LITRES (21/2 PINTS)

ROAST SPICED QUINCES

ROAST SPICED QUINCES
ROAST SPICED QUINCES

1 cup sugar
1 litre (1¾ pints) water
4 medium quinces, peeled, cored and halved
½ stick cinnamon
4 whole cloves
1 star anise
1 tablespoon orange blossom water
2 tablespoons lemon juice
4 sprigs fresh mint
1½ teaspoons ground cinnamon
1 tablespoon crushed pistachios
4 sprigs mint, to garnish

Preheat the oven to moderate, 180°C (350°F) Gas Mark 4.

In a pan, dissolve the sugar in the water over medium heat.

Place the quince halves in a large baking dish, making sure you leave some space between them.

Add the cinnamon stick, cloves, star anise, orange blossom water, lemon juice and mint to the dish.

Pour the sugar syrup over the top and cover with foil.

Bake for about 2½ hours, basting occasionally, or until tender and a dark pink colour is reached.

Place 2 quince halves in each bowl and spoon over a little syrup. Sprinkle over the cinnamon and pistachio and garnish with fresh mint.

Serve with cream or ice-cream.

SERVES 4

Lemongrass, saffron and rose are strongly flavoured so a little goes a long way, otherwise the fragrance can be overwhelming. Enjoy this beautiful, almost therapeutic dish.

LEMONGRASS, SAFFRON AND ROSE CRÈME BRÛLÉE

4 lemongrass sticks
Pinch saffron threads
1 teaspoon rosewater
1 litre (1¾ pints) cream
12 egg yolks
150g (2 oz) sugar

Soak the lemongrass, saffron and rosewater in the cream overnight to infuse.

Preheat the oven to very slow, 100°C (200°F) Gas Mark 1.

Mix the egg yolks and sugar until blended, then add to the infused cream.

Bake for 20 minutes.

MAKES 12 CUPS

ROSEWATER AND
PISTACHIO ICE-CREAM

ROSEWATER AND
PISTACHIO ICE-CREAM

100g (3½oz) shelled pistachios
500ml (16fl oz) cream
250ml (8fl oz) milk
½ vanilla bean
1 teaspoon prepared saffron
6 egg yolks
150g (5oz) caster sugar
2 tablespoons rosewater
1 cup water
1 cup sugar
7g (¼oz) edible dried rose petals

Preheat the oven to hot 220°C (450°F) Gas Mark 6.

Lightly toast the pistachios in the oven and once cooled roughly chop.

In a pan, bring the cream, milk and vanilla to the boil.

Turn the heat off and stir in the saffron, leave to cool down slightly. Beat the egg yolks and caster sugar together. Add the hot cream mixture slowly to the yolks, whisk, then cook in a clean pot over simmering water until thickened (should coat the back of the spoon), do not allow to boil. Remove, cool in an ice bath, and then add in the rosewater.

Strain through a sieve and leave in the fridge while you continue preparation.

To make the sugar syrup dissolve the sugar in the water stirring frequently, without allowing it to boil. Stop stirring, add the rose petals, and when the sugar has dissolved bring to the boil. Remove from heat and leave the petals to soak. When cool, use only 200ml (6fl oz) for this recipe.

Churn the cream mixture in an ice-cream maker for a few minutes before adding the rose petal syrup and the pistachios then continue churning until frozen.

If you don't have an ice-cream maker, place the cream mixture into the freezer for 20 minutes. Whisk the mixture then freeze for another 20 minutes, then add the rose syrup and pistachios and continue freezing and whisking on 20 minute intervals until the ice-cream holds its own shape. This shouldn't take much longer than 2 hours.

Serve with fresh orange segments.

MAKES 1 LITRE (13/4 PINTS)

SAFFRON AND CARDAMOM CARAMEL

600ml (20fl oz) milk
½ cup caster sugar
Pinch saffron threads
½ teaspoon cardamom seeds
2 tablespoons rosewater
1 tablespoon orange zest
4 beaten eggs

Caramel
½ cup caster sugar
¼ cup hot water
1 teaspoon strained lime juice

Preheat the oven to moderate 180°C (300°F) Gas Mark 4.

Heat the milk, sugar, saffron and cardamom in a saucepan until the milk starts to boil, then turn the heat off. Allow to cool down before adding the rosewater and zest of orange. Whisk while gradually pouring in the eggs. Set aside.

In a saucepan on medium heat, dissolve the sugar in the hot water without boiling, stirring occasionally. As it heats, brush the inside of the pan with pastry brush dipped in cold water to remove any sugar crystals that are splashed up.

Turn the heat to high and as bubbles emerge add the lime juice, boil rapidly without stirring until it reaches a medium caramel colour.

Pour the caramel sauce evenly into 6 crème caramel cups and allow to cool.

Whisk the milk mixture so it has no skin then fill up the cups.

Place on a deep oven tray. Fill the tray with water until it reaches ¾ of the height of the cups.

Bake in the oven for approximately 45 minutes to 1 hour, until firm.

Allow to cool for several hours or overnight.

To serve, tip upside down onto a plate allowing the sauce to run down the custard.

Garnish with fresh lime segments and raspberries.

MAKES 6 CUPS

SAFFRON BUTTERMILK PANNA COTTA

SAFFRON BUTTERMILK PANNA COTTA
SAFFRON BUTTERMILK PANNA COTTA

2 cups (500ml/16fl oz) fresh cream
1 cup (250ml/8fl oz) full cream milk
1 tablespoon prepared saffron
Zest from 1 lemon
6 egg yolks
$2/3$ cup of caster sugar
1 tablespoon rosewater
2 cups (500ml/16fl oz) buttermilk
6 gelatine leaves

Bring the cream, milk, saffron and lemon zest to boil in a saucepan.

Reduce the heat and simmer for 3 minutes, then remove from the heat.

In a bowl, whisk together the egg yolks, caster sugar and rosewater.

Add the buttermilk and gelatine, stir until the gelatine dissolves.

Pour the buttermilk mixture into the saffron cream saucepan and stir until combined
 and slightly cooled.

Lightly spray dariole moulds, coffee cups or short glasses with oil, pour in the panna cotta
mix and refrigerate overnight.

Serve chilled with the citrus salad.

MAKES 9 CUPS

Amlou is a traditional Berber nut paste not unlike peanut butter or tahini with a unique Middle Eastern flavour. It can be used as a spread for bread, a dip, in baking or even added to milk drinks. I prefer to use the traditional manual method which gives me a slightly chunky, coarse amlou.

AMLOU
MOROCCAN NUT PASTE

200g (6½oz) roasted and salted almonds
100g (3 oz) hazelnuts
250ml (8fl oz) argan oil
½ cup (125ml/4fl oz) honey

Crush the nuts in a mortar and pestle until you get a rough paste then slowly spoon in the argan oil and honey, one tablespoon at a time, then stir to thoroughly combine.

If you prefer a smoother amlou, grind the nuts in a food processor before adding the other ingredients as before.

Store in a sealed container at room temperature.

10–12 SERVINGS OF APPROXIMATELY 3 TABLESPOONS

A Moroccan custard dish which is usually shared in a large communal bowl, though you can serve it individually in small bowls or sundae glasses.

MEHALABEYA WITH *AMLOU*
MOROCCAN CUSTARD

MEHALABEYA WITH AMLOU

MOROCCAN CUSTARD

1 litre (1¾ pints) milk
¾ cup caster sugar
2 cinnamon sticks
¼ cup cornflour (corn starch)
½ cup almond meal
2 tablespoons orange blossom water
¾ cup amlou

Bring 750ml (24fl oz) of the milk to the boil in a large saucepan along with the sugar and cinnamon sticks.

Lower the heat and leave to simmer.

Meanwhile, mix together the cornflour, almond meal and remaining cup of milk in a bowl to achieve a smooth paste.

Add the paste to the simmering milk, then remove the saucepan from the heat.

Stir in the orange blossom water then strain into a jug or a large shallow bowl.

Either pour into individual glasses/bowls or leave in the large bowl to serve in a communal way. Seal with plastic wrap to prevent a skin forming and leave to cool to room temperature, then chill if preferred.

Before serving, spoon a generous amount of amlou on top for a nice combination.

SERVES 8

CHEBBAKIYA
MOROCCAN HONEY BISCUTS

1 teaspoon yeast
500g (1lb) plain flour
70g (2½oz) ground aniseed
150g (5oz) sesame seeds
80g (2¾oz) butter
1 egg
Salt, pinch
Sugar, pinch
½ teaspoon ground cinnamon
Saffron, pinch
100ml (3fl oz) orange blossom water
Oil
1kg (2lbs) honey
Arabic gum (see note), pinch

Dilute the yeast in 50ml (2fl oz) of warm water.

In a bowl, combine the flour, aniseed and half the sesame seeds then stir in the butter, egg, yeast water, salt and sugar.

Add in the cinnamon, saffron and just enough orange blossom water to achieve a dough. Knead well.

Divide the pastry into 2 balls and leave covered in a warm place for 10 minutes to rise.

Flatten the balls of dough to about ½cm (¼in) thickness before cutting it into 6 rectangles of approximately 9 x 4cm (3½x1½ins).

Make 4 slits in each rectangle at an even width apart so you have five 9cm (3½ins) strips that are still connected at the top.

Lightly pull up the 2nd and 4th strip and lightly pull the 1st, 3rd and 5th in the opposite direction, moulding the pastry into a cage-like circular shape.

Place the pastries on a dry clean surface until you've done them all.

Heat about 2cm (¾in) of oil in a large fry pan.

Carefully place each biscuit pastry into the hot oil, turning when necessary so they are golden brown all over. Remove from the oil and drain them on paper towels.

In the meantime place the honey, Arabic gum and any left over orange blossom water into a pan and bring to the boil.

Dip each cooked biscuit into the hot honey to completely coat, then leave to drain again on paper towels and sprinkle with the other half of the sesame seeds.

Serve at room temperature with tea or coffee.

MAKES 12

NOTE
Arabic gum is also known as *mastiha*, and can be bought at Asian or Middle Eastern grocers.

LIME AND PROMEGRANATE
CHEESECAKE

LIME AND POMEGRANATE
CHEESECAKE

200g (6½oz) wheatmeal biscuits
80g (2½oz) butter, melted
500g (1lb) cream cheese
175g (5½oz) caster sugar
1 tablespoon cornflour
3 eggs
4 limes, juiced
2 teaspoons ground cinnamon
1 teaspoon vanilla essence
Salt, pinch
1½ cups sour cream
75g (2½oz) roasted almond flakes

Pomegranate Topping
1 gelatine leaf
1 pomegranate
½ cup pomegranate couli
½ cup warm water

Preheat the oven to moderate, 180°C (350°F) Gas Mark 4.

Crush the biscuits in a food processor then place in a bowl and mix with the melted butter to achieve a hard paste. Press the biscuit mix into the bottom of a lined cake tin.

Beat the cream cheese and sugar together in a bowl until smooth, then add the cornflour, eggs, lime juice, cinnamon, vanilla and salt before adding the sour cream. Continue beating until well combined.

Sprinkle the almond flakes over the biscuit base and then pour in the cheese mixture.

Place the cake tin into a baking tray, fill the baking tray with water until it reaches halfway **up the** cake tin. This means the cake will cook very gently.

Bake for 45 minutes.

Take the cake out of the oven and allow it to cool for half an hour.

Meanwhile, soak the gelatine in the warm water until it dissolves.

Cut open the pomegranate and scoop out all the seeds into a bowl.

Mix the gelatine liquid with the pomegranate couli, stir well then add in the pomegranate seeds.

Pour the sauce over the top of the cake while it's still in the tin so that it holds its shape. Leave in the fridge for approximately 1 hour to set.

Take the cake out of the tin and serve in slices drizzled with extra couli and ice-cream on the side.

DRINKS

REFRESHING MINT TEA

Mint tea is the true expression of the famous Moroccan hospitality. It is a beautiful, fragrant, refreshing drink that soothes, calms and relaxes, or awakens and cheers.

Tea itself was only introduced to Morocco in the 18th century, spreading throughout the country during the mid 1800s as European trade with Morocco thrived. The story goes that the Sultan Moulay Ismail received abundant amounts of tea and sugar as gifts and compensation from the European diplomats in order to free European prisoners.

Moroccans took to tea, making it their own and adding it to the traditional hot drinks made from herbs and spices such as saffron, marjoram, absinthe and of course mint with hot water and sugar.

In Morocco, mint tea is all about the way it is served and what that represents. If you were just to hand someone a cup of tea that would be seen as rude, but to sit someone down, bring in the biscuits and dates that almost always accompany the tea, the tray with the pot, the glasses and sugar, and prepare the tea in front of your guest; then you have created a warm and welcoming atmosphere that is the essence of Moroccan hospitality.

People are always saying how no two Moroccan teas are ever the same, this is simply because no recipe is followed. However in my restaurant I have to be consistent to keep my customers happy. Follow this recipe and you will get the same result every time until you know how you really like it and then you can adapt it to your taste.

WINE

A Roman colony in antiquity, Morocco was once a major producer of wine, which was imported in large quantities to Rome. But at the beginning of the 8th century, the country converted to Islam which forbids the drinking of alcohol, so the vineyards producing grapes for winemaking were abandoned, leaving only those specialising in the growing of grapes for eating. It wasn't until the early 20th century after Morocco became a French protectorate that the wine producing vineyards were re-established.

Most Moroccan wines are red or rosé, the climate being unsuited to producing white wines. Varieties mainly consist of carignane, vin gris, grenache as well as a cabernet sauvignon, syrah, merlot and mourvedre. Some local bottles to look out for there are Guerrouane, Beau Vallon and Gris de Boulaoune as well as some local beer such as Casablanca, Stork, and Flag.

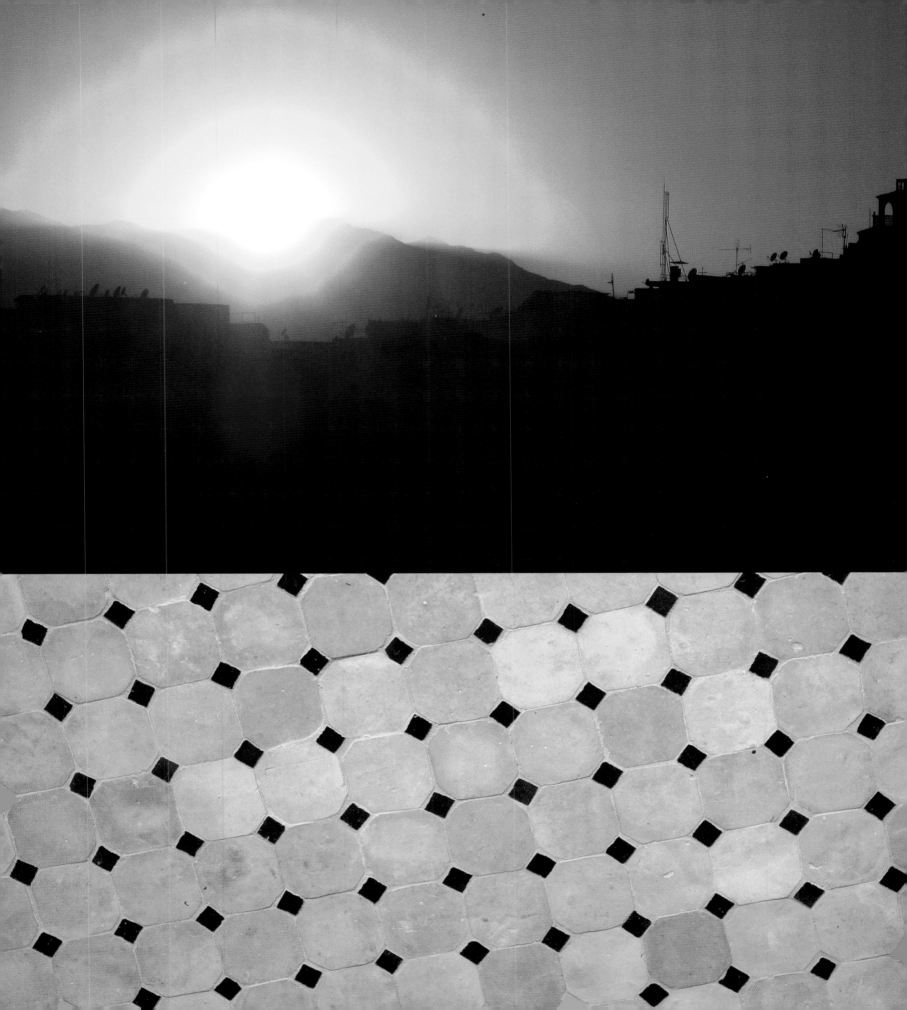

MOROCCAN MINT TEA

MOROCCAN MINT TEA
MOROCCAN MINT TEA

¼ cup Chinese gunpowder (or green) tea
1 litre (1¾ pints) boiling hot water plus 1 extra cup for washing the pot
1 bunch spearmint (preferably a short, curly bunch with red stalks), washed
¾ cup sugar

Place the tea into the pot and pour in the cup of boiling water, swish around then strain the water out leaving the leaves inside. This is the traditional way to clean the leaves and remove the bitterness.

Pour in the litre of boiling water and allow to boil for 1 minute over hot embers (or on the stove top).

Stuff the spearmint tightly into the pot and place back on the heat for a few more seconds.

Add in the sugar and allow to dissolve.

Using a tea towel to protect your hands, pour out a glass, then pour it back into the pot, repeat another two times, this allows the tea to properly mix and infuse. Try the tea first before serving to ensure it is well mixed.

Serve the tea into the other glasses, pour from high up and come down towards the end to create froth.

Be sure not to pour to the top, leave a rim of about 3 fingers deep for the person to hold the glass by. The person preparing the tea is the only person to pour until the pot is empty and each glass is to be handed to the right. These are the traditional guidelines for a mint tea 'ceremony', have fun with it and enjoy.

Serve in a large metal teapot.

SERVES 4
(2 glasses each, traditionally it is 3 each but see how you go)

Drinking Arabic coffee in Morocco is like drinking a pot of tea in Australia. Moroccans love to drink it sitting outside a café European style, whilst at home it's served as an occasional treat. Each household has its own blend, the spices vary. This recipe is for a sweet, spiced coffee with a perfume as strong as its flavour.

ARABIC COFFEE

1½ cups water
4 teaspoons Turkish (or any finely ground) coffee
2 teaspoons raw sugar
3 cardamom pods, cracked
1 clove
1 cinnamon stick

In a small saucepan, bring the water to boiling point before turning off the heat.

Add in the coffee, sugar, cardamom, clove and cinnamon stick and bring back to the boil. Keep boiling until the froth starts to rise then turn off the heat.

When the froth starts to dissolve and has settled, stir, then turn the heat back up again, allowing to boil and the froth to rise again.

Serve the coffee straight away with an equal share of the froth in each glass.

Allow to cool and settle for a moment before drinking.

Serve with Moroccan biscuits.

SERVES 4 IN SMALL GLASSES

INDEX OF RECIPES

PRESERVES, SAUCES, DIPS & DRESSINGS

Argan Oil   43–49

Beetroot Dip   59

Besara Green Pea Dip   58

Bruschetta and Dips   51–61

Carrot Dip   58

Lemons, Moroccan Preserved   138

Limes, Moroccan Preserved   133

Minted Labneh with Zaatar   124

Olives, Preserved   61

OOA (Out of Africa) Salsa   169

Peach, Plum and Pomegranate Sauce   184

Pomegranate Couli   183

Preserved Lemons and Limes   131–139

Tomato Concasse   75

MARINADES & SPICES

Charmoula Marinade   139

Dukkah   123

Harissa   109–119

Harissa, Green   112

Harissa, Red   114

Ras el hanout   124

Saffron   141–155

Spices   121–129

Zaatar   123

SOUPS & ENTRÉES

Anchovy and Bocconcini Bruschetta   57
Eggplant Bruschetta   52
Grilled Fig and Bastourma Bruschetta   54
Marinated Poached Tomato Bruschetta   53
Mixed Olives and Harissa Bruschetta   56
R'fissa Be Rezat El Kadi (Turban of the Judge)   35
Roasted Red and Green Capsicum Bruschetta   55
Semi-Dried Tomato and Smoked Salmon Bruschetta   54
Spicy Glazed Onion and Goats Cheese Bruschetta   53

BREAD & PASTRY

Bread and Pastry   31–41
Khobz (Moroccan Bread)   34
Medfouna (Berber-style Pizza)   41
Pastilla Belkhodra (Vegetable Pastilla)   39
Trid Be Rghaif   38

TAJINES

Breakfast Tajines   65–77
Cassoulet Tajine   85
Cheese Breakfast Tajine   76
Chicken Tajine with Figs and Walnuts   88
Chicken Tajine with Quince   94
Douara (Tripe, Heart and Liver Country Style Tajine)   89
Duck Tajine with Cumquat Confit and Glazed Turnip   91
Main Course Tajines   79–95
Merguez Concasse Breakfast Tajine   71
Quail and Goats Cheese Tajine with Braised Pickled Onions and Raisins   83
Rabbit Tajine with Saffron and Chickpeas   86
Sardine and Perch Kefta Tajine   84
Seafood Breakfast Tajine   68
Tajine of Mussels   80
Veal Knuckle Tajine with Artichokes   173
Vegetable Breakfast Tajine   66

MEAT & POULTRY

Harissa and Minted Yoghurt Baked Chicken with Sweet Potato   115
Merguez Sausages   74
Saffron Couscous with Lamb Shank and Tfaia   147
Tangia Marakechia   135

SEAFOOD

Artichoke Heart with Caramelised Scallops, Salmon and Beetroot Relish   176
Barbecued Baby Squid with Baba Ghanouj and Herb Salad   126
Fresh Scallops and Salmon with Creamy Brown Lentils   125
Moroccan Baked Fish   137
Saffron Mussels Cassolettes   153
Sardines Stuffed with Harissa Wrapped in Vine Leaves   116
Whole Baked Dukkah Barramundi with Red and Green Harissa   119

VEGETABLES, SALADS & ACCOMPANIMENTS

Artichokes   171–177
Baked Eggplant Timbale with Couscous, Crabmeat and Mascarpone Tapenade
     and Roast Capsicum and Tomato Sauce   102
Bastourma and Pomegranate Salad   167
Caramelised Tomatoes   165
Chekchouka (Roasted Bell Pepper and Tomato Salad)   162
Couscous   97–107
Couscous Preparation   100
Goats Cheese, Date and Fig Salad   161
Grilled Polenta with Glazed Parsnip and Pumpkin Sauce   48
Maakouda (Potato Croquettes)   129
Middle Eastern Salad   158
Pomegranates   179–187

Saffron Badinjal (Saffron Eggplant)   148
Saffron and Nut Rice   151
Salads   157–169
Sweet Cucumber Salad   164
Vine Leaf and Couscous Wrapped Salmon Filo   106

DESSERTS & CAKES
Amlou (Moroccan Nut Paste)   202
Chebbakiya (Moroccan Honey Biscuits)   206
Citrus Salad   193
Ginger Ice-cream   194
Lemongrass Saffron and Rose Crème Brûlée   196
Lime and Pomegranate Cheesecake   207
Mehalabeya with Amlou (Moroccan Custard)   205
Palets Au Saffron   155
Roast Spiced Quinces   195
Roasted Pear with Nut Crumble and Rose Pomegranate and Strawberry Sauce   187
Rosewater and Pistachio Ice-cream   198
Saffron Buttermilk Panna Cotta   201
Saffron and Cardamom Caramel   199

DRINKS
Arabic Coffee   217
Date and Orange Blossom Shots   190
Drinks   209
Mint Tea, Moroccan   214
Saffron Tea   154
Wine   212

First published in Australia in 2008 by
New Holland Publishers (Australia) Pty Ltd
Sydney • Auckland • London • Cape Town

www.newholland.com.au

1/66 Gibbes Street Chatswood NSW 2067 Australia
218 Lake Road Northcote Auckland New Zealand
86 Edgware Road London W2 2EA United Kingdom
80 McKenzie Street Cape Town 8001 South Africa

National Library of Australia Cataloguing-in-Publication entry

M'Souli, Hassan.

Make it Moroccan : modern cuisine from the place where the sun sets / Hassan M'Souli.

9781741106015 (hbk.)

Out of Africa (Restaurant)
        Cookery, Moroccan.
        Morocco--Description and travel--Pictorial works.

641.5964

ISBN 9781741106015

Publisher: Fiona Schultz
Publishing manager: Lliane Clarke
Editor: Kay Proos
Assistant writer: Jasmine M'souli
General photography: Hassan M'Souli
Supplementary travel photography: Jimmy Castrisos
Food photography and styling: Graeme Gillies
Food stylist: Najma Elyounsei
Staff photography: Ramahl M'Souli
Designer: Hayley Norman
Production: Liz Malcolm
Printer: Tien Wah Press, Singapore